INVESTING IN
MUNICIPAL
BONDS

INVESTING IN MUNICIPAL BONDS

BALANCING RISKS AND REWARDS

James J. Cooner

JOHN WILEY & SONS
New York • Chichester • Brisbane • Toronto • Singapore

Library of Congress Cataloging-in-Publication Data

Cooner, James J.
  Investing in municipal bonds.

  Bibliography: p.
  Includes index.
  1. Municipal bonds—United States. I. Title.
HG4952.C66   1987   332.63′233′0973   86-28911
ISBN 0-471-84941-3

Printed in the United States of America

10 9 8 7 6 5 4 3 2 1

To
Kathy

foreword

During the past three years, the annual volume of tax-exempt municipal securities has almost doubled from $119.2 billion to $223.4 billion in 1985, and the individual investor has replaced the commercial bank as the largest holder of these obligations. Now, with the latest revisions in the tax laws expected to curtail tax-exempt bond issuance sharply and make investing in these securities significantly less attractive for the banks, the individual will be playing an ever more important role in the future.

Prior to 1977, individuals made virtually all of their municipal bond purchases directly through their brokers—the big bond houses or dealer banks. It was mostly a game for the rich and those in the higher income tax brackets. But with inflation climbing steadily in the late 1970s and early 1980s, forcing salaries higher and pushing individual wage earners into more costly tax brackets, the tax-exempt market became a game for the less affluent investor to play as well.

These investors are using the tax-exempt unit trust funds and the open-end managed bond funds as their entrance into the municipal market. Although the unit trusts started up in 1961, they were not a significant factor in the market until the late 1970s. The open-end funds began operations in 1979. These two vehicles allow the smaller investor to buy tax-exempt bonds in lesser denominations.

Since individuals have come to the forefront as the largest holders of tax-exempt debt and the biggest buyers of new issues, a need has been created for a book to explain the various rewards and risks surrounding this type of investment for the nonprofessional buyer. *Investing In Municipal Bonds: Balancing Risks and Rewards*, written by James J. Cooner, fills this need.

In his book, Mr. Cooner unravels the mysteries of the municipal bond world and translates into simple language its technical terms. It is the most comprehensive text to be published since the passage of the 1986 tax reform package.

Mr. Cooner carries excellent credentials for writing a book

about municipal bond investing. He has more than 20 years of experience in this field, being employed by two major dealer banks and a nationally recognized investment banking firm. He is presently in charge of sales and marketing activities for the Personal Investment Counsel Division and its Tax Exempt Bond Department at The Bank of New York. He was previously at Kuhn, Loeb & Co. and prior to that at The Chase Manhattan Bank.

Currently a member of the faculty of the New School for Social Research, Mr. Cooner has also served on the faculty of the American Institute of Banking and has lectured at various schools and before numerous professional organizations. He has twice been chairman of the Education Committee of the Municipal Bond Club of New York. But most important of all, he has been a dedicated student of the municipal bond industry throughout his career.

Investing In Municipal Bonds: Balancing Risks and Rewards should be read by all individuals contemplating an investment in municipal bonds or currently holding municipal bonds in their portfolios.

WILLIAM J. RYAN

Associate Editor
The Bond Buyer

preface

This book is written for the individual who has $1000 to $100,000 to invest in municipal bonds. It will show you how to obtain a higher return from municipal securities either from your initial purchase or from better management of existing investments in municipal bonds.

The municipal bond market has become increasingly complex during recent years. In addition, the Tax Reform Act of 1986 has changed many rules concerning tax-sheltered investments. In simple, nontechnical language I will review the different types of municipal bonds available in the marketplace, pointing out the relative advantages and disadvantages of each for the individual investor. In addition, I will discuss the new tax codes as they apply to municipal bonds.

There are many practical suggestions in this book that will provide you with ideas that you can apply to your municipal investments, resulting in higher tax-free returns, reduced security risk, and a better municipal portfolio.

This book is based on my 20 years of practical experience in the municipal market. Over the years I have answered inquiries from thousands of investors just like you who want to reduce their taxes, increase their returns, and reduce their risks in investing in municipal bonds. This book brings together the answers to hundreds of questions that I have been asked repeatedly by investors on the job, in the classroom, and at my lectures and seminars.

Although this book is written primarily for the municipal bond investor, the contents will provide invaluable information for those who have an interest in all types of investments, students, professionals employed in the stock and bond markets, and financial representatives of state and municipal governments.

JAMES J. COONER

February, 1987

acknowledgments

I would like to thank the following business colleagues for their assistance: Myer R. Strauss, Vice President, Financial Guaranty Insurance Company; Marshall L. (Bud) Wilcox, Jr., Treasurer, Port Authority of New York and New Jersey; and Jack Zimmermann, Vice President, Van Kampen Merritt Inc. In addition, I want to thank my agent, Paul M. von Freihofer, for the encouragement that was needed to start this project.

contents

INVESTING IN
MUNICIPAL
BONDS

1

by way of
historical
introduction

Welcome to the exciting world of municipal bonds. Welcome to an investment arena that has experienced within the last 10 years gyrating interest rates, explosive growth, and well publicized defaults. Today a changing tax environment has added extra complications to investing in the tax-exempt bond market. In recent years the activity in the municipal market has intensified; the stakes are higher as more and more investors are drawn to municipal securities in their attempts to decrease their tax liabilities. Profit opportunities are now greater than they were in the past, but so are risks.

Now more than ever, the investor in municipal securities needs information not only about bonds themselves, but even more importantly, about how the municipal market functions. Obtaining this information has been extremely difficult for the majority of investors who are committing their investment dollars to municipal bonds. This book will fill this gap and provide the information you need to make better future selections of tax-exempt investments and to manage more effectively the municipal securities currently in your investment portfolio. Remember, no one has a greater stake in the success of your investments than you do. The greater your knowledge of municipal bonds and the bond market, the greater the probability of above average investment returns.

AND THE BONDS ARE OFF AND RUNNING . . .

Before we start our discussion, let's look back to see where it all started. The exact date of the first municipal bond as we know it today is not recorded. However, New York City, one of the best known issuers of municipal bonds, sold marketable municipal debt as early as 1812.[1] The earliest recorded problem faced by the municipal bond investor occurred in 1839 when Mobile, Alabama, defaulted on one of its bond issues.[2] The volume of municipal bonds outstanding during the 19th Century grew slowly; the total amount outstanding at the turn of the century was estimated at $1 billion for the entire country.[3] This figure of outstanding indebtedness pales in comparison to recent market activity: in April, 1985, New York State sold more than $4 billion of municipal notes in a single issue. Of course, municipal bond sales in the 19th Century were not stimulated by tax exemption because federal income taxes did not become a financial burden for most people until the early 1940s.

States and municipalities shifted their bond sales into a higher gear during the prosperous 1920s. The total amount of all outstanding bonds was about $1 billion at the start of the 20th Century, although each year during the 1920s saw annual bond sales in excess of that total number.

The stagnation of the 1930s and the demands of a total war economy during the first half of the 1940s combined to limit the growth of municipal financing for capital projects. During this period of approximately 15 years, annual bond sales averaged considerably less than during the decade of the 1920s. The dollar volume of bond sales in 1942 ($507 million), if adjusted for inflation, represented the lowest sales volume for any year in this century.[4]

At the conclusion of World War II, the country faced two changes that would influence the municipal bond market. First, the backlog demand for goods and services in general was reflected in the need for greater spending on municipal capital projects. Roads had to be built to get America to the suburbs, and when the suburbanites arrived, they needed schools, sewers, water, and hospitals to support the new communities. In addition to new capital projects, money was needed to repair and modernize existing physical plants that had been neglected during the Depression and war years. The second change was taxation. Whereas federal taxation had been a nominal factor for the average citizen in 1930, after the war a growing tax burden influenced many middle income and upper income taxpayers to make financial decisions that would legally lessen the impact of increased taxes.

Bond issues increased at a steady, predictable rate throughout the 1950s and 1960s. States and municipalities sold securities in a marketplace that was marked by few events that disturbed its tranquility. Interest rates were low, and bond price fluctuations were nominal.[5]

THE MUNICIPAL BOND MARKET SINCE 1970

The growth of municipal bond sales in the 1970s and 1980s was explosive. Figure 1.1 shows the tremendous increase in bond sales in recent years. The increase is due mainly to the growth of revenue bond financing, that is, bonds backed by a particular project or enterprise. From 1975 to 1984, revenue bonds jumped more than fivefold, whereas bonds backed by the taxing power of the states and municipalities—general obligation bonds—increased less than two fold.

During the past 10 years, three types of revenue bonds have

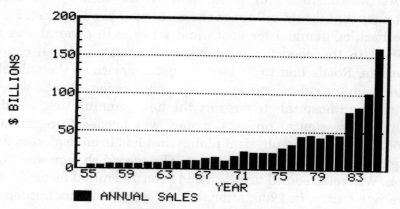

Figure 1.1   Bond sales. (Courtesy *The Bond Buyer*.)

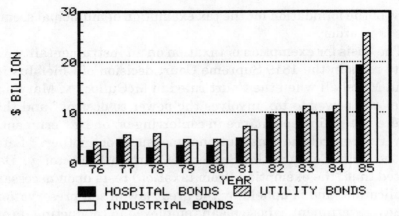

Figure 1.2 Types of revenues. (Courtesy *The Bond Buyer.*)

shown the greatest growth: Figure 1.2 shows the surge of hospital bonds, gas and electric utility bonds, and industrial development bonds. These bonds will be reviewed in detail later in this book. The changing nature of these categories of bonds also will be explored when we cover the question of new tax legislation, which will diminish the issuance of these types of bonds in the future.

The accelerated growth of bond sales in the early 1980s was associated with a period of historically high interest rates. Because interest rates represent the price needed to sell bonds in the marketplace, the increased volume of new bonds was one of the factors that lifted interest rates on tax exempt bonds to lofty double-digit returns during this period.

WHY ARE THEY TAX EXEMPT ANYWAY?

The current tax situation regarding municipal bonds will be discussed in detail in Chapter 7. But at this point, a historical review of the foundation for the tax exemption of municipal securities is in order.

The basis for exemption of taxation on an instrumentality of a state rests in the 1819 Supreme Court decision of Chief Justice John Marshall when the Court ruled in McCullock v. Maryland "that the power to tax involves the power to destroy" and that "there is a plain repugnance in conferring on one government a power to control the constitutional measures of another."[6] Later in the 19th Century the Supreme Court in Collector v. Day stated that "the exemption (from taxation) rests upon necessary implication, and is upheld by the great law of self preservation; as any government, whose means employed in conducting its operations, if subject to the control of another and distinct government, can exist only at the mercy of that government. Of what avail are these means if another power may tax them at discretion."[7]

In 1895, the Supreme Court again ruled in Pollock v. Farmers Loan & Trust Co. that "a municipal corporation is the representative of the state and one of the instrumentalities of the state government. It was long ago determined that the property and revenues of municipal corporations are not subjects of Federal Taxation . . . and that the tax in question is a tax on the power of the states and their instrumentalities to borrow money, and consequently repugnant to the Constitution."[8]

When the Federal Income Tax Law was adopted in 1913, the interest income from municipal bonds and notes was excluded from taxation by the Federal Government. This exclusion has been incorporated in various revisions of the tax law; the 1954 revision, for example, specifically excludes from gross income the interest received "from obligations of a state, a Territory, or a possession of the United States, or any political subdivision of any of the foregoing."[9]

During the 1920s, the Supreme Court once again considered the question and ruled in favor of tax exemption. In National Life Insurance Co., v. United States, the Court held that "it is settled doctrine that directly to tax income from securities amounts to taxation of the securities themselves . . . the United States may not tax state or municipal obligations."[10]

In 1941, the Internal Revenue Service attempted to tax the interest on the bonds of the Port Authority of New York on the argument that the Authority was neither a state nor a municipality. The United States Court of Appeals ruled in Commissioner of Internal Revenue v. Estate of Shamberg "that the interest on the bonds issued by the Port Authority of New York was exempt from federal income tax because it was interest on bonds of a political subdivision of a state within the statutory exemption."[11]

The United States Treasury itself has stated that "since the beginning of the income tax, the Internal Revenue laws have provided that interest on obligations of States, territories, possessions of the United States, any political subdivisions of the foregoing . . . has been excluded from the gross income of any holder of these obligations."[12]

But times change. The recently passed tax regulations will result in some investors having a tax liability on some of their municipal bond interest. Chapter 7 will address in detail the question of the current tax regulations regarding municipal bonds.

WHO ARE THE BUYERS OF MUNICIPAL BONDS?

All classes of investors, both individual and institutional, who purchase municipal securities are motivated by their tax environment. High taxes stimulate actions to avoid the impact of the taxes. Investors who are not subject to a tax burden—pension funds and charitable institutions, for example—have little interest in municipal bonds or notes as an investment vehicle.

The three principal classes of investors in the tax-exempt market are: individual investors, commercial banks, and casualty insurance companies. Historically, the banks and casualty insurance companies accounted for the bulk of the purchases of

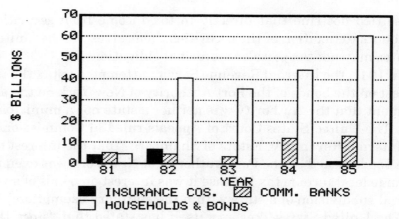

Figure 1.3 Annual purchases of municipal bonds. (Courtesy Salomon Brothers, Inc, "Prospects for Financial Markets in 1986," p 53.)

newly issued municipal bonds. In recent years, however, the importance of the individual investor has grown dramatically and the importance of the banks and insurance companies has declined. This fact is shown by Figure 1.3. In 1985, approximately one-half of all bonds coming to market were directly purchased by individuals. In addition, approximately one-quarter were purchased by municipal bond funds and unit investment trusts. Because these funds and trusts act mainly as proxies for individual investors, individuals purchase either directly or indirectly at least three-quarters of all newly issued municipal bonds. The Federal Reserve Bank estimates that individuals hold more than $0.5 trillion of municipal bonds, or approximately 46% of all tax-exempt bonds outstanding.[13] The growing importance of the individual investor has changed the way municipal bonds are marketed: witness the growth of insured bonds and bond funds. These and other developments will be discussed in detail later.

It is interesting to contrast what has been happening in recent years in the municipal bond market with what has happened in the equity market. The role of the individual investor has grown to primary importance in the tax-exempt market, whereas the role of the individual has diminished in the stock markets. Today the institutional investor dominates the equity market, whereas the individual investor is the primary source of funds for newly issued municipal bonds. The importance of the individual investor has very definite implications for the future direction of the tax-exempt market, because innovations involving new types of securities, credit enhancements, and market acceptance of newly issued bonds and notes will all have to take the investment objectives of the individual investor into account.

2

birth of a bond

Much activity takes place before a newly issued municipal bond is made available to investors in the marketplace. Planning for a bond sale may begin anywhere from one to two years before the bonds are actually sold by the state or municipality.

What is a municipal bond? A municipal bond is a debt obligation issued by a state, a municipal subdivision of a state, or a state or municipal authority, whereby the bond issuer promises to pay the bondholder interest on a periodic basis and to pay the face value, or principal, of the bond at maturity. Municipal bonds are similar to bonds issued by the United States Government, corporations, and foreign governments; the main difference between municipal bonds and other bonds is the special tax status that is associated with the interest you receive from municipal bonds.

A municipal bond represents a loan. When you invest in a newly issued municipal bond, you are lending money to the municipality that issued the bond. The bond instrument that the investor receives is the evidence of the loan. The borrowed money will be used to construct a capital project, such as a school or bridge. If you loan money to a municipality, you do not have any ownership position in the issuer's assets; if the municipality can not repay the loan, that is, the municipal bond, you can not claim a portion of the school or bridge that was built with the money raised by the sale of the municipal bonds.

ENTER THE MUNICIPAL BOND ISSUER

Let's follow the activity that occurred before the sale of one particular bond that was issued on June 26, 1985, by the Port Authority of New York and New Jersey. As I review the development of this issue, let's examine some of the characteristics that apply to all tax-exempt bonds.

Who is the issuer of this particular bond? The Port Authority owns and operates a number of transportation and other facilities of commerce in and around New York harbor. It is nearly impossible to move in or out of the New York Metropolitan Area without using the facilities of the Port Authority. The Port Authority operates the major New York airports, the bus terminal, and all the bridges and tunnels linking New York and New Jersey. Most of the ship traffic entering the New York harbor uses the marine terminals of the Port Authority. In addition, the Port Authority owns and operates the World Trade Center and the Port Authority Trans-Hudson rail system. In total, this Authority operates more than 30 major facilities shown on Figure 2.1. The total amount of the Port Authority's capital investment in facilities is more than $5 billion, and its activities are spread over an area of 1500 square miles, an area larger than the state of Rhode Island.

Obviously, the needs of the Port Authority to raise money through bond sales are much more complex than the needs of a local school district selling bonds to build a new gym for the community's high school. The size and frequency of the borrowing may be very different, but the actions preceding the bond sale are similar both for a major issuer of bonds, like the Port Authority, and for a local school district.

Upward to a year before the sale, various departments of the Port Authority develop financial plans which include new facilities and capital improvements. These plans are submitted to the Port Authority's Board of Commissioners; the approval by this board will result in the authorization for a bond sale. In the case of the Port Authority, any authorizations for bond sales also must be approved by the governors of both New York and New Jersey.

Whenever the amount of money that is needed builds toward the $100 million level, the financial officials of the Port Authority start preparing a bond sale. The Port Authority likes to sell bonds so that the size of any one bond issue will be between $100 and $200 million. The capital needs of this huge municipal authority are so great that a bond sale under $100 million would

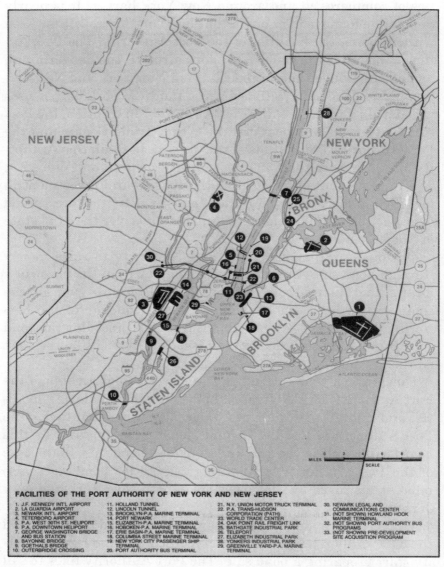

FACILITIES OF THE PORT AUTHORITY OF NEW YORK AND NEW JERSEY

1. J.F. KENNEDY INT'L AIRPORT
2. LA GUARDIA AIRPORT
3. NEWARK INT'L AIRPORT
4. TETERBORO AIRPORT
5. P.A. WEST 30TH ST. HELIPORT
6. P.A. DOWNTOWN HELIPORT
7. GEORGE WASHINGTON BRIDGE AND BUS STATION
8. BAYONNE BRIDGE
9. GOETHALS BRIDGE
10. OUTERBRIDGE CROSSING
11. HOLLAND TUNNEL
12. LINCOLN TUNNEL
13. BROOKLYN-P.A. MARINE TERMINAL
14. PORT NEWARK
15. ELIZABETH-P.A. MARINE TERMINAL
16. HOBOKEN-P.A. MARINE TERMINAL
17. ERIE BASIN-P.A. MARINE TERMINAL
18. COLUMBIA STREET MARINE TERMINAL
19. NEW YORK CITY PASSENGER SHIP TERMINAL
20. PORT AUTHORITY BUS TERMINAL
21. N.Y. UNION MOTOR TRUCK TERMINAL
22. P.A. TRANS-HUDSON CORPORATION (PATH)
23. WORLD TRADE CENTER
24. OAK POINT RAIL FREIGHT LINK
25. BATHGATE INDUSTRIAL PARK
26. TELEPORT
27. ELIZABETH INDUSTRIAL PARK
28. YONKERS INDUSTRIAL PARK
29. GREENVILLE YARD-P.A. MARINE TERMINAL
30. NEWARK LEGAL AND COMMUNICATIONS CENTER
31. (NOT SHOWN) HOWLAND HOOK MARINE TERMINAL
32. (NOT SHOWN) PORT AUTHORITY BUS PROGRAMS
33. (NOT SHOWN) PRE-DEVELOPMENT SITE ACQUISITION PROGRAM

Figure 2.1 Facilities of the Port Authority of New York and New Jersey. (Courtesy The Port Authority of New York and New Jersey.)

not be an efficient way to raise money; a sale too much over $200 million may create problems of trying to raise too large an amount of money at one time in the bond market.

Informal discussions were held between the financial representatives of the Port Authority and major municipal bond underwriters who would be bidding on the bond issue to determine current market conditions, interest rates, and the general climate for selling a major issue of Port Authority bonds. About this time, the Port Authority determined the maturity structure of the bonds, that is, the year or years in which the bonds would become due.

Municipal bonds are sold in two different maturity structures: serial bonds and term bonds. Serial bond issues have bonds maturing each year over a number of years. Each segment of the bond issue has a specific maturity, and investors can purchase bonds with a maturity that meets their particular portfolio needs. A term bond issue has only one maturity. All the bonds in a term bond issue have the same maturity date; however, term bonds usually have call features and sinking funds which result in many of the term bonds being called for redemption before their stated maturity date.

THE OFFICIAL STATEMENT

Approximately one month before the bond sale, an official statement will be prepared for potential bidders and investors. The official statement is a booklet that will describe the new bond issue in detail; the official statement shows the maturity structure of the issue, call features, and security provisions. Additionally, the official statement will contain information about the current financial status and future plans of the issuer. A very important feature of the official statement will be a discussion of the tax status of the interest that the municipality will pay to the bond investors.

An official statement is prepared for nearly every bond issue that will be offered for sale to the investing public. The length of this booklet will vary from 100 pages or more for the official statement of the planned issue of the Port Authority to 25 pages or so for a typical local school bond issue. The official statement is used primarily by the municipal bond underwriters who will bid on the issue and by municipal bond analysts who will review the issue and assign a bond rating.

If you want a copy of an official statement for a new bond issue, the municipality selling the bonds or your bond dealer will supply you with one. Current regulations require that the municipal bond dealer who sells you a newly issued tax-exempt bond must provide you with a copy of the official statement, or a summary thereof, if one is prepared by the issuing municipality. However, the official statement is often written in technical and legal terminology that can be difficult to understand.

THE RATING AGENCIES AND BOND RATINGS

Bond ratings are an important guide for the investor to use to determine the general quality of a municipal bond. There are two major agencies that rate municipal bonds: Moody's and Standard & Poor's. Both use a series of letters to distinguish between bonds of various quality grades. Moody's ratings range from a top rating of "Aaa" to a low rating of "C"; Standard & Poor's also uses alphabetical designations ranging from "AAA" to "D". Appendix A describes the various rating categories in detail.

Armed with the official statement, the Port Authority's representatives will visit the bond rating agencies to make a presentation about the forthcoming issue. This presentation will attempt to show the bond issuer to be in strong financial condition so that the forthcoming bond issue will receive the highest possible rating. The higher the rating, the better the acceptance by investors and the lower the interest cost that the Port Authority will have to pay on the bonds. The bond analysts who work for the rating agencies will hear the presentation, receive the information and material provided by the Port Authority, and start the analytic process that will result in a bond rating in a few days. The issuer of the bonds pays the rating agencies' fees to have the bonds rated.

After making the presentation at the rating agencies, the Port Authority representatives await the ratings to be assigned to the forthcoming bond sale, hoping of course for a high rating for the new bond issue. Analysts working for the rating agencies may be in contact with the Port Authority's financial staff for clarification of data about the Port Authority's financial status and future borrowing plans. A day or so before the bond sale scheduled for June 26th, Moody's rated the issue an "A1" and Standard & Poor's assigned an "A+". These very respectable ratings confirmed the ratings that had been assigned to previous issues of the Port Authority's bonds.

FORM OF THE BONDS

Two or three weeks before the bond sale, the Port Authority will provide a copy of the bond for the new issue to the bond printers. All the particulars about the bond instrument can be prepared for printing except the interest rate, which will be determined at the time of sale.

The Port Authority bonds will be issued as registered bonds. A sample of a registered bond is shown in Figure 2.2. A registered bond shows the name of the owner and the number of bonds, or the par value, represented by the bond certificate. The registered bond looks very much like a common stock certificate. If you own a registered bond, a bank will be appointed to be the bond's paying agent, and this bank will mail you an interest check twice a year. The amount of the check will be a function of

Figure 2.2 Registered bond, City of Philadelphia.

18

the par value of the bonds and its interest rate. The terms interest rate and coupon are used interchangeably in the bond market; both terms have exactly the same meaning. For example, the $25,000 par value of City of Philadelphia bonds shown in Figure 2.2 have an interest rate of 10.25% and would pay $2562.50 in interest each year ($25,000 × 10.25%); each semiannual interest payment received by the bondholder would be $1281.25 (one-half of $2562.50).

Before July 1, 1983, nearly all municipal bonds were issued in coupon form. If you invest in a coupon bond, you will receive a bond certificate similar to the one shown in Figure 2.3. A coupon bond has two parts: the bond instrument itself and a series of coupons. This form of bond does not show the name of the owner, and it is payable to the bearer. For this reason, coupon bonds are also called bearer bonds. Every six months, the investor would remove the coupon that has become due from the bond; this coupon represents the semiannual interest payment. The coupon would be deposited in a bank account in the same manner as you would deposit a check.

Coupon bonds are still available in the secondary or resale market; however, because municipal bonds are no longer being issued in coupon form, and because older, outstanding municipal bonds are always being retired upon the bonds' maturity or their call, the availability of coupon bonds will be continually diminishing.

What are the advantages and disadvantages of each form of bond? The registered bond is a much safer instrument because it is registered in the name of the owner. The receipt of interest by check is a much simpler process than clipping and processing coupons twice a year. Furthermore, because the names of the owners of the bonds appear on the books of the bank that acts as the transfer agent, the issuer is able to contact the owners of the bonds if information must be disseminated about bond calls or about changes in the bond indenture (which is a contract between the issuer and the investors that is administered by a bank trustee).

No. A

No. A

THE ATLANTIC COUNTY IMPROVEMENT AUTHORITY

CONVENTION HALL ADDITION LEASE-RENTAL BOND, SERIES A

DUE DECEMBER 1, 1978

THE ATLANTIC COUNTY IMPROVEMENT AUTHORITY (hereinafter called the "Authority"), a public body politic and corporate organized and existing under and by virtue of the laws of the State of New Jersey, for value received, hereby promises to pay, solely from the funds and revenues of the Authority pledged therefor as hereinafter described, to the bearer or, if this bond be registered as herein provided, the registered owner hereof, on the FIRST DAY OF DECEMBER, 1978, the principal sum of

FIVE THOUSAND DOLLARS ($5,000)

and to pay, solely from said funds and revenues, interest on such principal sum from the date hereof at the rate of

FIVE AND NINETY HUNDREDTHS PER CENTUM (5.90%)

per annum, payable semi-annually on the first days of June and December in each year until the Authority's obligation with respect to the payment of such principal sum shall be discharged as provided in the Resolution hereinafter mentioned; but only in the case of an interest coupon upon presentation and surrender thereof as they severally become due. The interest so payable, and the principal of and redemption premium, if any, on this bond are payable upon presentation and surrender of the respective coupons therefor annexed hereto and upon presentation and surrender of this bond, will be payable at the principal office in the Borough of Manhattan, City and State of New York, of Chemical Bank New York Trust Company, or, at the option of the holder, at the principal office of The First National Bank, in the City of Atlantic City, New Jersey, in any coin or currency of the United States of America which at the time of payment is legal tender for the payment of public and private debts.

This bond is one of a duly authorized issue of Convention Hall Addition Lease-Rental Bonds of the Authority (herein called the "Bonds"), issued and to be issued under and pursuant to a resolution of the Authority duly adopted and entitled "Resolution Authorizing the Issuance of Convention Hall Addition Lease-Rental Bonds" (herein called the "Resolution"). As provided in the Resolution, the Bonds may be issued from time to time in one or more series in various principal amounts, may mature at different times, may bear interest at different rates and may otherwise vary as in the Resolution provided. The aggregate principal amount of Bonds which may be issued under the Resolution is not limited except as provided in the Resolution. Bonds issued and to be issued under the Resolution are and will be secured by the pledge of funds or revenues provided therefor.

The Bonds are issuable in the form of coupon Bonds in the denomination of $5,000 and in the form of registered Bonds without coupons in the denomination of $5,000 or any integral multiple of $5,000. Coupon Bonds, upon surrender thereof at the principal office of the Trustee with all unmatured coupons and all matured coupons for which top payment or only partial payment has been provided attached, may, at the option of the bearer and in the manner and subject to the conditions and upon the payment of the charges provided in the Resolution, in like manner, subject to such conditions and upon the payment of such charges, registered Bonds may be exchanged for coupon Bonds or for other registered Bonds of the same series, duly executed by the registered owner or by his duly authorized attorney. The Bonds are transferable by the registered owner thereof, in person or by his attorney duly authorized in writing, at the principal office of the Trustee with a written instrument of transfer satisfactory to the Trustee, duly executed by the registered owner or by his duly authorized attorney, and thereupon a new registered Bond or Bonds, and in the same aggregate principal amount of coupon Bonds of the same series, maturity and interest rate with appropriate coupons attached, or registered Bonds without coupons of the same series, maturity and interest rate of any other authorized denominations.

The Series A Bonds maturing on or before December 1, 1983 are not subject to redemption prior to maturity. The Series A Bonds maturing on December 1, 1984 are subject to redemption by or on behalf of the Authority, prior to maturity and upon published notice as hereinafter set forth, on or after December 1, 1983, as a whole at any time or in part from time to time on any interest payment date, at a redemption price equal to the principal amount of each Bond or portion thereof to be redeemed, together with interest accrued to the date of redemption, and the redemption premium (if any) expressed as a percentage of the principal amount, set opposite such period in the following table:

From	To	Premium
December 1, 1983	November 30, 1985	4%
December 1, 1985	November 30, 1988	3%
December 1, 1988	November 30, 1991	2%

(Both dates inclusive)

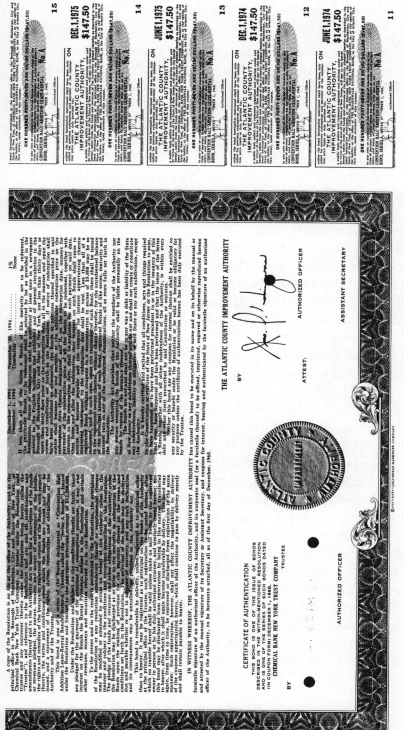

Figure 2.3 Coupon bond, The Atlantic County Improvement Authority.

Coupon bonds have the advantage of ease of transfer. You can transfer a coupon bond to another person as easily as you can transfer a dollar bill: you simply give the bond to a second party. This ease of transfer also creates a security problem for the holder of coupon bonds. You must treat coupon bonds as you would cash. These bonds must be kept in a safe deposit box or held in a custodial account by your bank or broker. If coupon bonds are lost or stolen, the investor will face a long and expensive process to have them replaced. Even the small coupons themselves are bearer instruments. Handle the coupons the same way you would handle cash.

Despite these security problems, some investors prefer to hold municipal bonds in coupon form. These investors may take comfort in the fact that their name does not appear on any records as the beneficial owner of the bond. If you don't like to have your name recorded as the owner of an investment, coupon municipal bonds may be for you.

The change from coupon to registered bonds occurred in mid-1983 as a result of provisions of the Tax Equity and Fiscal Responsibility Act of 1982. This legislation closed what the federal government perceived to be a loophole, whereby the transfer of municipal bonds in coupon form provided an opportunity for evading estate, inheritance, and gift taxes. With this change, many participants in the municipal market predicted that a two-tiered bond market would develop, with coupon bonds commanding a substantial price premium over registered bonds. This never happened. Coupon bonds are still traded in the secondary market with no meaningful price differentials to registered bonds. However if you wish to invest in tax-exempt bonds in coupon form, you should act quickly—the supply of these bonds is constantly being reduced.

The most recent trend in the municipal market is to have bonds issued in book entry form. If you purchase a book entry bond, you will not receive any bond instrument at all; you receive only a confirmation stating that you are the owner of the bond. All the records about the bond issue and its owners are held in a computer of a bank or a security depository agent.

TYPE OF BOND UNDERWRITING

Let's return to the Port Authority. The issuer's financial officials must decide on the method to be used to sell the bonds to the underwriters. Will the Port Authority offer the bonds at competitive sale and sell the entire $100 million issue to whomever is willing to pay the best price for the bonds in the competitive marketplace? Would it be more advantageous to the Port Authority to enter into a negotiated sale with one group of bond underwriters and try to hammer out an attractive price for the bonds with just one group of dealers?

When the Port Authority sells a bond issue, it is selling a product, namely its debt obligations. The Port Authority, like the seller of any product, wants to get the best price for what it is selling. But what is the "price" of the bonds from the viewpoint of the issuer? The price is the rate of interest that the bonds will bear. For example, if bidder A is willing to buy the Port Authority bonds at an 8.5% interest rate, and if bidder B wants the bonds for an 8.75% interest rate, the Port Authority will sell the bonds to bidder A because 8.5% represents a lower interest cost and therefore a better price for the issuer.

For the June 1985 transaction, the Port Authority chose to sell the bonds by competitive bidding. The Port Authority expected to get a better bid from a competitive sale than from a negotiated one because market conditions were favorable for selling bonds, interest rates had been declining, and underwriters had been bidding very aggressively for new bond issues. In addition, although this was a large bond issue, it was a relatively simple one; the bonds would be term bonds with only one maturity, and there would be no unusual redemption or conversion features. This issue would be an example of "plain vanilla" bonds. If the bond issue had been a very large issue or if it had contained any unusual features that required extra selling efforts on the part of the underwriters, the Port Authority might have considered a negotiated sale.

THE LEGAL OPINION

During this time, the legal department of the Port Authority prepared various legal documents related to the pending sale. In addition, an outside firm of attorneys, called bond counsel, was employed by the Port Authority to review all the legal aspects of the bond sale; bond counsel examined the laws under which the issuer operates to assure that there were no legal impediments to prevent the sale and to make certain that the bonds could indeed be issued. When the bonds were sold, bond counsel issued a legal opinion which states that the bonds are legal and binding obligations of the Port Authority. In addition, the legal opinion discusses the tax status of the bond's interest payments.

The municipality that issues bonds should choose a law firm to act as bond counsel that is recognized by the marketplace as having expertise in the field of municipal finance law. A legal opinion issued by a recognized law firm protects the investor from suffering a potential financial penalty by purchasing an illegally issued security. The legal opinion is an integral part of the bond instrument itself. Today most municipal bonds have the legal opinion printed right on the bond. However, many older bonds have the legal opinion attached to the bond as a separate document; if you own bonds with a separate legal opinion, and if you want to sell the bonds in the secondary market, you must deliver a copy of the legal opinion with the bonds you want to sell. If you can not deliver the legal opinion, the bonds will be sold "ex legal" and you will receive a lower price for the bonds you are selling.

OTHER PARTIES

Negotiations will take place between the Port Authority and various banks to select the registrar, the paying agent, and the bond trustee. These banks provide a variety of services to both the bondholders and the issuer as long as the bond issue is still outstanding.

The registrar will maintain records of the investors who own the bonds. The initial purchasers of the new issue will be recorded by the registrar, and as these bonds are bought and sold in the secondary market after their initial sale, the registrar will continually update the records of ownership.

After the bonds are sold, as each semiannual interest payment is due, the Port Authority will advance the funds to pay the interest to the bank acting as the issue's paying agent. The paying agent will send interest checks to the bondholders shown on the books of the registrar. Many times the same bank acts as both the registrar and the paying agent for a bond issue.

The bank that acts as the trustee for the bond issue verifies that the issuer is fulfilling all the terms of the bond resolution or indenture. The trustee will be required, among other things, to make certain that the money raised through the sale of bonds is being properly used, that insurance is being maintained on the facilities, and that reserve funds are at proper levels. The trustee acts as a watchdog on behalf of the bondholders to insure that the issuer of the bonds complies with all the terms of the bond contract.

RECEIVING THE BIDS

The day has arrived for the sale of the bonds. The Port Authority has completed all the work necessary to sell the bonds: the issue has been advertised for sale, the official statements have been distributed, and the bond ratings are in place.

A few minutes before 11:00AM on June 26, 1985, the treasurer of the Port Authority received three sealed bids from three competing groups or syndicates of municipal bond underwriters. Each bid proposed the terms under which each syndicate would buy the entire $100 million bond issue from the Port Authority. One bid, presented by a syndicate headed by Dillon, Read & Co., offered to buy the bond issue if the interest rate or coupon would be 8.70%; this bid proposed to pay $98,050,000 to the Port Authority for the $100,000,000 bond issue. If the Port Authority accepted this bid, the interest cost for the Port Authority would be 8.771%. The two other syndicates both proposed a coupon of 8.75% and overall interest rates of 8.812% and 8.817% for the Port Authority's bonds. The three bids were all quite close to each other; this would be expected in a competitive sale of bonds by a well-known issuer like the Port Authority.

The Port Authority chose the bid made by Dillon, Read group of underwriters because it represented the lowest interest cost for the bonds. A formal award was soon made and the bonds were offered for sale to investors.

Let's look at that Dillon, Read syndicate bid again. The underwriters were willing to pay the Port Authority $98,050,000 for $100,000,000 par value of bonds. The difference of $1,950,000 represents the profit the underwriters hope to make on this transaction because the bonds will be offered for sale to investors at par value. In dollar terms $1,950,000 appears to be a large profit, but it represents less than 2% of the total dollar value of the transaction.

The Port Authority still has to complete a few actions before the bond transaction is finished from the issuer's viewpoint. Based on the terms of the winning bid, the Port Authority provides the bond printers with the interest rate information. The bonds can now be printed and the finalized copies of the official statement can be prepared which will have all the information about the bond issue, including the interest rate determined by the competitive sale. Approximately two weeks after the sale, the Port Authority delivers $100 million of bonds to the underwriters who submitted the best bid. The underwriters pay the bid price for the bonds to the Port Authority and continue to sell and distribute the bond issue.

This chapter has reviewed the activity that must be undertaken by various parties before a bond is available for purchase by the municipal bond investor. In the next chapter, we will discuss the activity in the new issue market for tax-exempt bonds and suggestions on how you can improve your investment decisions in the new issue market.

3

the primary
or new issue
market

When a municipality has made the decision to sell bonds, the sale takes place in the primary or new issue market. As we have seen in the preceding chapter, the entire issue of municipal bonds will be sold as a package of securities to a group of municipal bond dealers.

As an investor you must be aware of one very important aspect about municipal bonds owned by dealers. Some investors regard their securities with awe as if the securities were some type of icon or relic. I have met investors who actually speak reverently about their bond holdings. On the other hand, dealers may speak with reverence about the securities they are offering for sale to investors, but the bond dealers' greatest reverence is for the money that the investor will spend to buy the bond the dealer is trying to sell. In the new issue market, an issue of municipal bonds is like any other product or commodity in the hands of the seller: mark it up in price, sell it to a retail buyer as quickly as possible, and move on to sell something else. If you appreciate the fact that bonds are really commodities for the dealer, you will understand much better how the primary market for municipal bonds functions.

NEGOTIATED VERSUS COMPETITIVE SALES

Bonds are sold to dealers by states and municipalities by two different methods: through competitive bidding between rival groups of dealers and through a negotiated sale to one group of dealers. Figure 3.1 shows that, in dollar terms, there has been a shift in recent years toward more bonds being sold by negotiation and less by competitive bidding.

In a negotiated sale, the municipality contracts with a small number of bond underwriters, called the managers, to form a larger group of bond underwriters to purchase the entire bond issue from the municipality. The combination of the small number of managers and the larger group of underwriters is called a

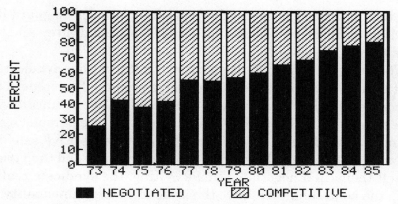

Figure 3.1 Types of sales. (Courtesy *The Bond Buyer*.)

syndicate. The managers will propose a tentative purchase price to the municipality for the bond issue, and the entire syndicate will start developing orders for the bonds from investors based upon the tentative pricing. As orders are received by the managers, the correctness of the proposed bid is put to the test: if too few orders are developed, that is, the "book" is too small, the bonds will have to be repriced more attractively for the investors; if the "book" is reasonably strong, the correctness of the tentative bid is confirmed.

A few days later, the syndicate buys the issue from the municipality. A negotiated sale of a bond issue represents reduced risk for the syndicate because the syndicate members have had several days to test the price of the bonds with prospective investors. Only when the pricing seems to lead to a profitable conclusion to the transaction will the issue actually be purchased from the issuing state or municipality.

Let me compare a negotiated sale with a competitive bid transaction. In a competitive sale, two or more rival syndicates will be formed to bid on the bond issue. Most bond issues sold at competitive bidding will attract from three to six bids. The rival syndicates will submit sealed bids to the issuing municipality at the time and place of sale. Each syndicate will closely guard its bidding strategy and reoffering price levels until after all the bids have been submitted.

The pressures of competition acting on the various syndicates will typically result in more aggressive pricing of an issue sold at competitive bidding than one purchased by one syndicate via a negotiated sale. The risk factor for the syndicate purchasing a municipal bond issue is much greater in a competitive sale: in the competitive sale, the syndicate buys the bonds and then tries to sell them; in a negotiated underwriting, the syndicate really sells the bonds and then buys the issue from the municipality.

BENEFITS OF A NEGOTIATED SALE

Are there differences for the individual investor between negotiated and competitive sales? Negotiated sales tend to result in newly issued bonds that have better returns for the investor. Bonds sold in the primary market via negotiation generally give a higher yield to the investor than do those sold at competitive bidding. This is because successful bidders must be willing to pay a somewhat higher price for bonds sold at competition in order to buy the issue away from competing syndicates. This higher bid price translates into a higher reoffering price, and lower yields for the investor buying the bond. One of the first rules of bond investing is the higher the price you pay for a bond, the lower will be the yield. The spread in prices and yields between bonds sold at competitive sale and via negotiation will not be great, but the spread is there and investors should be aware of it.

Another factor making bonds sold via negotiation more attractive to buyers arises from how the interest rates, or coupons, are assigned to the various maturities of the bond issue by both methods. In a competitive sale, the bidding syndicates usually must offer to pay at least par, or 100, for the entire bond issue. If the issuing state or municipality receives a par bid for the bonds, the syndicate must sell some or all of the bonds at a price over par to show profit in the transaction. This will require some portion of the bond issue to be priced at a premium over par. If the bond is a serial bond issue with bonds maturing over a number of years, the bonds in the earlier maturities of an issue, approximately the first five to eight years, will be priced at premiums. The premium pricing is required to provide the anticipated profit margin for the underwriters. Never forget that bond dealers are underwriting bond issues to make money and not simply to help communities raise capital. The premiums on bonds sold at competitive bidding make these bonds less attractive to many investors. If a term bond—that is, an issue with only one maturity—is sold at competitive bidding, the syndicates are usually able to bid somewhat less than par for the bonds so that the bonds can be offered at par to investors. This was the case with the Port Authority bond issue discussed earlier. However, serial bonds sold at competitive bidding will usually be priced at premiums for the earlier maturities.

By way of contrast, in a typical negotiated sale the syndicate will buy the bond issue at a discount from the municipality. In this case the securities could be either serial bonds or term bonds. The markup from the discount bid to par provides the profit for the syndicate. This allows all the securities to be offered in the primary market at par, a more attractive pricing mechanism for most investors.

How do you know if an issue is being brought to market via competition or negotiation? Simply ask your bond dealer. If the dealer doesn't know or seems reluctant to discuss this question with you, find a different bond dealer.

SPREADS IN THE NEW ISSUE MARKET

How does the bond dealer make money in the new issue market? If the newly issued bonds are sold either by competitive bidding or negotiation, the syndicate buys the entire bond issue from the

FIGURE 3.2. Typical New Issue Gross Spreads in Dollars per $1000 Bond

Rating	Spread
Competitive Bond Sale: 1 to 20-year General Obligation	
Aaa	$ 7.00
Aa	8.00
A	10.00
Baa	17.00
Negotiated Bond Sale: Long-Term Revenue Bond Issue	
Aaa	$11.00
Aa	13.00
A	20.00
Baa	25.00

municipality. Most municipal bond issues will be comprised of a package of various maturities. The various maturities will be sold to investors who have an interest in bonds maturing in a specific year in the future. The bond issue resembles an orange: the syndicate buys the issue (the orange) and then can pull the issue apart and sell bonds from various maturities just as you can pull the various sections of an orange apart from one another. Reoffering prices or yields are assigned to various maturities to produce a profit for the dealers who are members of the underwriting syndicate. Gross profit margins depend on a variety of factors, including the complexity of the securities, market conditions, average maturity of the issue, and quality of the bonds. Figure 3.2 shows typical gross spreads for bonds of different quality. The gross spread covers a number of costs associated with the bond underwriting and the profit that will be made by the individual syndicate member for selling the bonds to the investor. Anywhere from 50% to 75% of the dollar spreads shown in Figure 3.2 will be paid directly to the syndicate member who sells the bonds to the investor. By using the data in Figure 3.2, you can get an approximation of the profit the dealer is making from the sale of newly issued bonds to you. For example, suppose you purchase $20,000 of newly issued "A" rated, long-term revenue bonds. Figure 3.2 shows a gross profit in this type of issue of approximately $20.00 per $1000 bond. Your dealer will make about $10.00 to $15.00 profit per bond for selling the securities to you. On your purchase of $20,000, the selling profit would be between $200 and $300.

ADVANTAGES OF BUYING IN THE NEW ISSUE MARKET

There are several advantages for the investor of purchasing bonds in the new issue market, regardless of whether the bonds were brought to market by negotiation or by competitive bidding. The pricing mechanism is much more open and therefore fairer and more equitable than is the case in the secondary market. Bond issues are priced to reflect current market conditions and not the whim of some bond dealer. The buyer, especially the inexperienced bond investor, can expect to have securities offered at more competitive prices in the primary market than is often the case in the secondary market.

The investor who wants to buy bonds at par, as opposed to buying bonds priced at premiums or discounts, will find the supply of bonds offered at par to be much greater in the new issue market.

Because many new issues of municipals are huge issues of hundreds of millions of dollars, new issues are often priced more attractively with greater yields and lower prices than comparable bonds in the secondary market. This is due to basic supply and demand considerations. If a large quantity of bonds must be sold and cleared from the market, the price must be attractive enough to attract the buyers to purchase the bonds. The same principal applies to any commodity be it widgets or tax-exempt bonds. Remember, bonds are nothing but a commodity in the hands of the dealer.

Lastly, the new issue market gives the best call protection features for the investor. Call protection reduces the possibility that the state or municipality issuing the bond will redeem the bond before maturity. Municipal bonds typically are callable starting about 10 years after their issuance. If you are concerned about having bonds called from you, and the alternative of buying discount bonds with their accompanying lower cash flow doesn't appeal to you, the primary market will give you the best chances of maximizing the period you will hold your bonds without having them called away from you before maturity.

FINDING OUT ABOUT NEW ISSUES

Many financial periodicals and major newspapers list forthcoming municipal bonds. For example, each Monday, *The Wall Street Journal* lists a schedule of municipal bonds to be sold that week. The schedule also breaks the forthcoming issues down into those to be sold at competitive sale and those to be offered via negotiation. If you see the name of a bond on the schedule that interests you, contact your bond dealer to get more information about the issue. In addition, many bond dealers publish lists of forthcoming issues and information about new issues for distribution to their clients. Regardless of the source of information, if you have an interest in investing in a newly issued bond, I recommend that you take action sooner as opposed to later. The positive features of buying in the new issue market—fair pricing, par bonds, available quantity, and call protection—all favor the buyer who makes a decision to invest now rather than procrastinating.

Another source of information about the new issue market is the "tombstone ad." These ads for securities are called tombstones because the ad is usually bordered in black as would be the case for death notices. Tombstone ads not only have information about one particular new issue, but if you know how to interpret the ad, you also can learn about general conditions in the municipal market. These tombstones appear on a regular basis in *The Wall Street Journal* and the financial sections of other leading newspapers.

Look at Figure 3.3 illustrating a typical tombstone ad, in this case for a State of New York general obligation bond issue. This ad is similar to ones you will see appearing in newspapers at various times. The top portion, indicated A, shows the rating, some tax information, and the name of the issuer. The next portion, B, would normally have information about the dated date, that is, the date the bonds start to pay interest, when payments will be made, the paying agent bank that will be disbursing the interest payments, and any call features that may exist for the bonds. All this information is descriptive and important for decision making on the part of the investor.

The next portion, C, is of primary concern for the investor. Here we see how the bond issue is structured: the number of bonds maturing each year, the coupon or interest rate assigned to each year, and the yield to maturity for each year. The yield to maturity is the return the investor will receive for each maturity segment of the bond issue. This portion of the tombstone can be analyzed by any investor to determine relative market conditions in the tax-exempt bond market. The tombstone ad will allow you to see the risks and rewards associated with investing your funds in different maturities in any market condition.

Let me show you how this can be done. We will use the New York State issue shown in Figure 3.3 as our sample. Using a piece of graph paper, plot the years to maturity on one axis (Figure 3.4A) and yields on the other axis (Figure 3.4B). Next plot each yield from the tombstone ad with its corresponding maturity. For example, the 1991 maturity on the tombstone yields 7.00%; because the dated date is October 15, 1985, the October

NEW ISSUE

Ratings: Moody's: A
Standard & Poor's: A+

$160,000,000
State of New York
Serial Bonds

$92,500,000 Rebuild New York Through Transportation Infrastructure Renewal Bonds
$36,500,000 Environmental Quality Bonds
$14,000,000 Energy Conservation Through Improved Transportation Bonds
$12,000,000 Pure Waters Bonds
$5,000,000 Rail Preservation Bonds

Dated: October 15, 1985   Due: October 15, as shown below

Interest on the Bonds will be payable on April 15, 1986 and semi-annually thereafter on the fifteenth day of October and April of each year by check mailed to the registered owner. Principal will be payable at the principal office of The Chase Manhattan Bank, N.A., Fiscal Agent, New York, New York, or any successor Fiscal Agent. The Bonds will be issued as fully registered bonds in the denomination of $5,000 or integral multiples of $5,000.

The Bonds are subject to redemption prior to maturity.

Amount	Due	Coupon	Yield	Amount	Due	Coupon	Yield	Amount	Due	Coupon	Yield
$11,360,000	1986	9.60%	5.00%	$2,990,000	1996	8.00%	8.00%	$2,000,000	2006	8.75%	8.95%
11,360,000	1987	9.60	5.60	2,990,000	1997	8.10	8.15	2,000,000	2007	9.00	9.00
11,360,000	1988	7.75	6.20	2,990,000	1998	8.30	8.30	2,000,000	2008	9.00	9.00
11,360,000	1989	6.60	6.60	2,990,000	1999	8.40	8.40	2,000,000	2009	9.00	9.00
11,360,000	1990	6.80	6.85	2,990,000	2000	8.50	8.50	2,000,000	2010	9.00	9.05
11,360,000	1991	7.00	7.00	2,290,000	2001	8.50	8.60	2,000,000	2011	9.00	9.05
11,360,000	1992	7.25	7.25	2,290,000	2002	8.50	8.70	2,000,000	2012	9.00	9.05
11,360,000	1993	7.50	7.50	2,290,000	2003	8.75	8.80	2,000,000	2013	9.00	9.10
11,360,000	1994	7.70	7.70	2,290,000	2004	8.75	8.85	2,000,000	2014	9.00	9.10
11,360,000	1995	7.80	7.85	2,290,000	2005	8.75	8.90	2,000,000	2015	9.00	9.10

(Interest accrued from October 15, 1985 to be added)

The Bonds will be general obligations of the State of New York, and the full faith and credit of the State of New York will be pledged to the payment of the principal of and interest on the Bonds.

Bonds of particular maturities may or may not be available from the undersigned or others at the above prices on or after the date of this announcement.

The Bonds are offered when, as and if issued and subject to receipt of an opinion by the Attorney General of the State of New York that the Bonds are valid and enforceable obligations of the State See Exhibit A in the Official Statement. The Bonds will be available for delivery on or about October 17, 1985. The offering of these Bonds, is made only by means of the Official Statement, copies of which may be obtained in jurisdictions in which this announcement is circulated from such of the undersigned or other brokers or dealers as may lawfully offer these securities in such jurisdiction.

Merrill Lynch Capital Markets

Bankers Trust Company

Dillon, Read & Co. Inc.

Irving Trust Company

Roosevelt & Cross
Incorporated

Salomon Brothers Inc

North Star Bank
Albany

Langdon P. Cook & Co.
Incorporated

Underwood, Neuhaus & Co.
Incorporated

Citicorp Investment Bank
Citibank, N.A.

The First Boston Corporation

Donaldson, Lufkin & Jenrette
Securities Corporation

Goldman, Sachs & Co.

PaineWebber
Incorporated

Continental Bank
Continental Illinois National Bank
and Trust Company of Illinois

Chemical Bank

Manufacturers Hanover Trust Company

Ehrlich-Bober & Co., Inc.

Matthews & Wright, Inc.

Securities Corporation of Iowa

Stephens Inc.

E. F. Hutton & Company Inc.

Smith Barney, Harris Upham & Co.
Incorporated

First Chicago
The First National Bank of Chicago

The Bank of New York

October 3, 1985

Figure 3.3   Tombstone ad, State of New York.

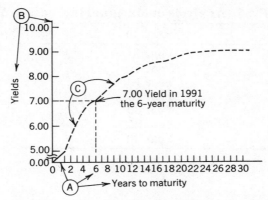

Figure 3.4   Yield curve analysis, $160,000,000 New York State general obligation bonds.

15, 1991 maturity is the six-year maturity for this issue. After you plot all the points and connect them, the resulting curve, C, is the yield curve for this issue of bonds. You can do the same procedure with any tombstone ad for a municipal bond issue with serial maturities.

Now you can analyze this yield curve and find out at what maturity you may want to make your investment. The longer the maturity, the greater the market risk should interest rates start to rise causing bond prices to fall. This risk is counterbalanced by greater returns being obtained from bonds with longer maturities than from bonds with shorter maturities.

The yield curve in the example is positively sloped for the first 20 years; after that, the yield curve becomes flat. This indicates that you are getting a higher and higher return on your money as you invest further and further out in time through the first 20 years. Notice that the yield curve rises at a faster rate from one through 10 years than it does from 11 to 20 years. You are receiving a better return on your money for extending an additional year in the one to 10-year range than you would receive for extending an additional year in the 11 to 20-year range. Af-

FIGURE 3.5. Analysis of Marginal Increase in Yields

Going from	Going to	Yield Increase
Year 0	Year 1	5.00%
Year 1	Year 5	1.85%
Year 5	Year 10	1.00%
Year 10	Year 15	.65%
Year 15	Year 20	.40%
Year 20	Year 25	.15%
Year 25	Year 30	.05%

ter 20 years, however, your increase in return is very small for additional extensions of maturities. There is little incentive for the investor to buy this particular bond with a maturity in excess of 20 years based upon the analysis of this yield curve.

Figure 3.5, which is based on the tombstone ad, shows the increased yields received for various time periods for the State of New York issue. This table shows that if you go from year 15 to year 20, you would increase your yield .40% or 40 basis points. A basis point equals one one-hundredth of a percentage point. If you extend your investment from year 20 to year 25, you increase your yield only 15 basis points. A further extension from 25 to 30 years increases yields an insignificant five basis points. As you extend your investment further and further out in time, which is an increase in risk, you are receiving smaller and smaller increases in yield which is your reward. Analyzing yield curves will give you an appreciation of this risk—reward relationship; you can easily analyze a yield curve if you know how to read and interpret a tombstone ad.

The sample I have used is for one particular issue at one point in time in the municipal market. Obviously, market conditions are always changing, yields and yield curves are changing, and the relative risks and rewards of investing are changing. But if you follow this example and apply it to a current tombstone ad, you will see not only what the current municipal market is returning investors for different maturities but the relative risk and reward associated with various maturities. The investor is going to have a better combination of higher returns and lower risks by staying in those portions of the yield curve that are positively sloped. Getting the little extra return for investing in longer term bonds may look enticing, but the extension is not worth the risk for most investors.

Let's return to the tombstone ad shown in Figure 3.3. The tombstone gives a brief description of the security of the bond, indicated by D. The security for this issue is quite simple because it is a full faith and credit general obligation bond of a state. If this were a more complicated revenue bond issue, investors would have been referred to the official statement for a more detailed description of the security provisions. Finally, the tombstone would indicate, E, the source of the legal opinion that will attest to the validity of the bond issue, when the bonds will be delivered by the syndicate members to the investors, and the names of the bond dealers who are members of the underwriting syndicate.

POINTS TO REMEMBER ABOUT THE PRIMARY MARKET

1. The new issue market provides a more honest and open pricing mechanism than exists in the secondary market.

2. Negotiated new issues tend to give you a higher return than new issues sold at competitive bidding.

3. The dollar pricing of bonds in the new issue market will generally be more attractive to municipal investors.

4. Analyzing a tombstone ad gives you information about a bond, yields available for various maturities, and relative risk—reward relationships existing in the market. If you know how to interpret a tombstone ad, you can gain quite a bit of information about overall market conditions for tax-exempt bonds.

4

the secondary
market

USED BONDS
FOR SALE

EFFICIENCY, BUT WITH RESERVATIONS

The secondary market for municipal bonds is the place where the investor goes to purchase bonds after their original offering in the new issue market, or where the investor goes to sell municipal securities before they mature. Liquidity—the ability to convert an investment into cash—is provided by the secondary market.

Investors are familiar with the working of the stock exchanges; these exchanges are examples of secondary markets. The image of the New York or the American Stock Exchange is one of efficiency and modernity. Brokers meet at one place to buy and sell a given stock. A bell rings to start trading activity in the morning and rings again in late afternoon to announce the close of trading. A transaction takes place and it is immediately recorded. The price of the transaction is made known to all interested parties by almost instant electronic communication. The next day the investor can see the details of the trading activity: how many shares traded, the high, the low, and the close. A secondary market open for all to see, with one central location: it's all so simple and so efficient.

By way of comparison, the secondary market for municipal bonds functions more like a cross between an oriental bazaar and a Charlie Chaplin movie.

The modern, electronic equipment in the secondary municipal market is primarily the telephone. Either by dialing or direct push-button line, the telephone links the approximately 500 dealers who comprise the secondary market for municipal securities. There is no central location: dealers are located from Maine to Miami and from Manhattan to Malibu. Most dealers, however, are concentrated in the large money market centers. There are no set trading hours for buying and selling municipal bonds. There is no recording of transactions. There is no record of the prices at which municipal bonds are traded. There are no electronic flashes and blips to show that a transaction has taken place. There is nothing. Don't flip open your morning paper to see how your State of California 8's of '97 traded the day before because, with one small exception that we will explore in this chapter, the newspapers do not record anything about transactions in the municipal market.

If the absence of information and data about transactions and prices of municipal bonds causes you to have some worry about the efficiency of the operations of the secondary market for tax-exempt securities, you are perfectly justified in your concern. If I had to choose a motto for the foggy municipal secondary market, it would be a toss up between "Let the buyer beware" and "What the market will bear."

THE BLUE LIST

After the telephone, the primary tool that the municipal bond dealer uses in the secondary market is a publication called *The Blue List*. *The Blue List* is published every business day by a division of Standard & Poor's Corporation. It is printed on blue paper—hence, its name—with blue ink—hence, to reinforce the name. Dealers throughout the country phone *The Blue List* with bonds they are offering for sale and with the prices they are asking for the bonds. For a fee of about $1.00 per line, the bonds appear offered for sale the next day for the nationwide community of municipal bond dealers. *The Blue List* does not record the sale of any bond; it does not reflect any actual transactions; it is only an indication that a dealer is pricing bonds for sale. *The Blue List* reflects availability and offering prices that are already one day old.

A good analogy to *The Blue List* is the classified section of your newspaper. In the classified there are houses, used cars, and secondhand furniture offered for sale at a price. If these used items actually could be sold at the printed price shown in the classified section—or "traded" to use the jargon of the bond market—then the items would no longer be listed because they would have been sold. If the classified section of the newspaper has used goods for sale, *The Blue List* has used bonds for sale, and many times the prices in *The Blue List* are as good a gauge of true value as are the prices in the classified section. Some dealers call *The Blue List* the "wish list" because they wish they could sell their bonds at the prices that they have inserted in *The Blue List*.

Does this mean that *The Blue List* can't be of value to the individual investor? No, *The Blue List* can be of great value. The first trick for the investor is to obtain a copy of this elusive publication. Ask your bond dealer or stock broker for a copy; it can be a few days old and still be a useful guide to the investor who wants to see what bonds are floating around in the secondary market.

But wait: just because you have a copy of *The Blue List* doesn't mean that you have hit a home run. You have to know how to decipher the hieroglyphics of *The Blue List*. Figure 4.1 shows a copy of the cover page of *The Blue List*, and Figure 4.2 shows a copy of one of the interior pages. Let's look at how to interpret the numbers on the copy of *The Blue List* illustrated in Figure 4.2.

The first line, marked A, shows the following entry:

75 N.J. TPKE. AUTH.
REV. 5.75 1/1/09 89 DLLNREAD

The "75" indicates the number of bonds that the dealer is offering, in this case $75,000 face value or par value. Next comes the name of the bond issue: New Jersey Turnpike Authority Revenue Bonds. The middle column shows the coupon or interest rate of the bond, namely 5.75%. The maturity date of January 1, 2009 follows. The bond is being offered at a dollar price of 89 by Dillon, Read.

The Blue List
of Current Municipal Offerings

(A Division of Standard & Poor's Corporation)

Published every weekday except Saturdays and Holidays by
The Blue List Publishing Company, 25 Broadway, New York, N. Y. 10004
Telephone 212 208-8200
Reg U S Patent Office • Printed in U S A

The bonds set forth in this list were offered at the close of business on the day before the date of this issue by the houses mentioned, subject to prior sale and change in price. Every effort is made by The Blue List Publishing Company and the houses whose offerings are shown in The Blue List to avoid mistakes and inaccuracies, but due to the fact that many offerings come in by wire and that the list is published after the offering houses have closed for the day, occasional errors are unavoidable. Neither The Blue List Publishing Company nor the offering houses take responsibility for the accuracy of the offerings listed herein.

+ Items so marked did not appear in the previous issue of The Blue List.
* Prices so marked are changed from previous issue.
c Items so marked are reported to have call or option features. Consult offering house for full details.

ANNUAL SUBSCRIPTION RATE (approximately 250 issues): Hand Delivery (Wall Street Area) $470.00; First Class Mail $605.00

AMT. M	SECURITY	PURPOSE	RATE	MATURITY	YIELD OR OFFERED PRICE	BY
	ALABAMA					
370	ALABAMA HIGHWAY AUTH.		8.25	9/ 1/87	4.50	PORTER
65	ALABAMA HIGHWAY AUTH.,ETM		4.50	2/ 1/88	4.75	CHEMICBK
+ 160	ALA.,HSG.FIN.AU.	O/Y 10.625	0.000	10/ 1/14	9.90	MERRILNY
500	ALA.ST.MUN.ELEC.AU.PWR.RV.		5.50	9/ 1/89	5.25	PRUBAATL
100	ALA.ST.MUN.ELEC.AU.PWR.RV.		6.70	9/ 1/92	6.00	FTRBIRMS
2000	ALA.ST.MUN.ELEC.AU.PWR.RV. (P/C 3/1/97 @ 100)		7.75	9/ 1/01	7.30	DREXELNY
50	ALA.ST.MUN.ELEC.AU.PWR.RV.		7.75	9/ 1/01	101	ACEDWROS
350	ALA.PUB.SCH.&COL.AU.RFDG.A		7.30	11/ 1/92	5.80	WITSHOCK
400	ALA.PUB.SCH.&COL.AU.		7.50	11/ 1/93	6.00	HUTSHOCK
1000	ALA.PUB.SCH.&COL.AU.		7.70	11/ 1/94	6.20	HUTSHOCK
160	ALA.PUB.SCH.&COL.AU.		6.75	11/ 1/00	6.80	SHATKLEE
30	ALA.PUB.SCH.&COL.AU.		6.75	11/ 1/00	6.90	SHATKLEE
20	ALA.PUB.SCH.&COL.AU.		7.75	11/ 1/01	7.00	OPCOFTL
+ 15	ALA.,ST.DOCK DEPT.RV P/C @ 103		6.75	11/ 1/03	7.10	OPCOFTL
1150	ALA.ST.DOCK DEPT,RV,HOSP,RV,		10	10/ 1/00 C95	7.85	SHEARNYB
25	ALABAMA SPL.,CARE FAC.HOSP.RV. (O/P @ 100)		4.75	7/ 1/96 C87	4.90	SHEARNTS

AMT. M	SECURITY	PURPOSE	RATE	MATURITY	YIELD OR OFFERED PRICE	BY
	ALABAMA-CONTINUED					
+ 100	BIRMINGHAM	P/C @ 102	9.75	10/ 1/05 C95	7.00	PRUBAATL
95	BIRM.-JEFF.CVC.CTR.AU	MBIA	7.50	9/ 1/04	7.00	FTRBIRMS
200	BIRM.-JEFF.CVC.CTR.AU (CA @ 96.15%)	MBIA	0.000	9/ 1/06	7.50	MOSLYNY
785	BIRM.-JEFF.CVC.CTR.AU (CA @ 88.90)	MBIA	0.000	9/ 1/07 C06	7.50	MOSLYNY
+ 170	BIRM.-JEFF.CVC.CTR.AU	MBIA	7.75	9/ 1/09 *	7.10	FIRBIRMS
450	BIRM.-JEFF.CVC.CTR.AU (CA @ 102)	MBIA	7.80	9/ 1/10 C96	7.20	BROWNNY
250	BIRM.-JEFF.CVC.CTR.AU	MBIA	7.80	9/ 1/10 *	7.10	FIRBIRMS
500	BIRMINGHAM MED.CO.BD.		6.625	4/ 1/00	7.00	POLLOCKW
10	BIRMINGHAM W/W BD.RV.		4.80	7/ 1/87	4.50	MOORESCH
25	CORTLANDT IDR		5.75	11/ 1/97	91	PORTER
100	COURTLAND IDR(CHAMPION INT,)		5.75	11/ 1/97	93	BARRBROS
25	COURTLAND IDR(CHAMPION INT,)		5.75	11/ 1/97	89	BEARSTER
30	COURTLAND I.D-R (CHAMPION INTL)		5.75	7/ 1/97	88	MABON1DB
600	DOTHAN	ETM	6.20	9/ 1/06	6.60	BEARSTER

THE BLUE LIST
OF CURRENT MUNICIPAL OFFERINGS

Volume 204 Number 43

August 29 1986 Friday

Figure 4.1 The Blue List of current municipal offerings (cover). (Sample provided by Standard & Poor's, Blue List.)

	Amount	Issuer		Coupon	Maturity		Price	Dealer
(A)	75	N.J.TPKE. AUTH REV.	ETM	5.75	1/ 1/09		89	DLLNREAD
	50	N.J.TPKE. AUTH REV.		5.75	1/ 1/09	C	87	GLICKEN
	25	N.J.TPKE. AUTH REV.		5.75	1/ 1/09		89	PAINEwNR
	50	N.J.TPKE. AUTH REV.		5.75	1/ 1/09		90	RYANBECK
	25	N.J.TPKE. AUTH REV.		5.75	1/ 1/09		86	SMITHBRT
	25	N.J.TPKE. AUTH REV.		6.75	1/ 1/09		94	BARRBROS
	50	N.J.TPKE. AUTH REV.		6.75	1/ 1/09		97	BEARSTER
	50	N.J.TPKE. AUTH REV.		6.75	1/ 1/09		96 1/2	RYANBECK
	100	N.J.TPKE. AUTH REV.		6.75	1/ 1/09		93	SMITHBRT
	50	N.J.TPKE. AUTH REV.		5.70	5/ 1/13		90	BEARSTER
	50	N.J.TPKE. AUTH REV.	ETM	5.70	5/ 1/13		88	DLLNREAD
(E)	50	N.J.TPKE. AUTH REV.	ETM	5.70	5/ 1/13		89	NEWBOLDw
	25	N.J.TPKE.AUTH.REV.	ETM	5.70	5/ 1/13		89 1/2	RYANBECK
	100	N.J.TPKE.AUTH.REV.		5.70	5/ 1/13		86	SMITHBRT
	100	N.J.TPKE. AUTH REV.	ETM	5.70	5/ 1/13		90	BARRBRUS
	50	N.J.TPKE. AUTH REV.		6	1/ 1/14		91	BEARSTER
	100	N.J.TPKE. AUTH REV.		6	1/ 1/14	C	89	GLICKEN
	50	N.J.TPKE. AUTH REV.		6	1/ 1/14		91	PAINEwNR
	50	N.J.TPKE. AUTH REV.		6	1/ 1/14		93	SMITHBRT
	100	N.J.TPKE. AUTH REV.		7	1/ 1/14		99	BEARSTER
(B)	50	N.J.TPKE. AUTH REV.		7	1/ 1/14	★	100	JOSEPHCO
	20	N.J.TPKE. AUTH REV.		7	1/ 1/14		97	RYANBECK
	50	N.J.TPKE. AUTH REV.		7	1/ 1/14		95	SMITHBRT
	125	N.J.TPKE. AUTH REV.		7	1/ 1/14			SMITHBRT
	1000	N.J.TPKE. AUTH REV.		5.625	1/ 1/18		4.10	SMITHBNT
		(MAND.PUT 10/1/86 @ 100)						
	10	N.J.TPKE. AUTH REV.		6.65	1/ 1/18	C88	5.50	SHEARNTS
		(MAND. @ 100)						
	25	N.J.TPKE.AUTH.REV.		7	1/ 1/18		6.00	ROGERSLB
		(PUT 11/1/89 @ 100)						
	500	N.J.TPKE.AUTH.REV.		7	1/ 1/18		6.00	SMITHBNT
		(MAND.PUT 11/1/89 @ 100)						
	140	N.J.TPKE.AUTH.REV.		7.10	1/ 1/18	★	6.25	SMITHBRT
		(PUT 4/2/90 @ 100)						
	20	N.J.TPKE.AUTH.REV.		7.10	1/ 1/18	★	6.25	SMITHBRT
		(PUT 7/2/90 @ 100)						
+	250	N.J.TPKE.AUTH.REV.	PUT @ 100	7.10	1/ 1/18	C90	6.25	SMITHBRT
	20	N.J.TPKE.AUTH.REV.		7.10	1/ 1/18		5.75	SHEARNTS
		(PUT 1/2/90 @ 100)						
	750	ATLANTIC CO.		7	8/ 1/87		4.60	CITIBANK
	435	ATLANTIC CO.		7	3/ 1/88		5.00	CHEMICBK
	50	ATLANTIC CO.	GEN.IMP.	7	3/ 1/90		5.75	MOORESCH
	100	ATLANTIC CO.	★REG★	7	3/ 1/92		6.00	STOEVERG
	495	ATLANTIC CO.		7	3/ 1/95		6.60	CITIBANK
	175	ATLANTIC CO.		7	3/ 1/96		6.70	OCNYMUN
	150	ATLANTIC CO.		7.10	3/ 1/97		6.80	OCNYMUN
	25	ATLANTIC CO.	CA @ 102	8	12/ 1/02	C94	6.90	PURCELL
	750	ATLANTIC CO.IMP.AU.		6.25	7/ 1/20		100 3/4	DWRNY
		(MAND.PUT 8/15/89 @ 100)						
+	60	ATLANTIC CO.UTIL.AU.SWR.RV.		6.875	1/ 1/12		6.90	FIRMONSE
		(ETM) (B/B)						
	400	AVALON BORO	MBIA	6.90	8/ 1/88		5.00	MARINNYC
	200	AVALON BORO		6.90	8/ 1/89		5.40	MARINNYC
	400	AVALON BORO		6.90	8/ 1/90		5.80	MARINNYC
	400	AVALON BORO	MBIA	6.90	8/ 1/91		6.00	MARINNYC
	220	AVALON BORO	MBIA	6.90	8/ 1/95	N/C	6.40	COOGANGI
	30	BAYONNE	ST.AID	9.10	5/ 1/99		7.00	RADLISEC
+	50	BERGEN CO.		4.80	7/15/87		4.25	SMITHBRT
	20	BERGEN CO.	★REG★	6.60	8/15/89		5.00	MOORESCH
	400	BERGEN CO.		6.60	8/15/90		5.30	CHEMICBK
(C)	25	BERGEN CO.		8	6/ 1/93		6.25	STIFELFI
	100	BERGEN CO.		6.60	8/15/93		6.00	FIRWISC
	195	BERNARDS TWP.		6.625	8/ 1/89		5.25	ROGERSLB
	550	BERNARDS TWP.		6.625	8/ 1/90		5.50	ROGERSLB
	155	BERNARDS TWP.		6.625	8/ 1/91		5.75	ROGERSLB
	15	BERNARDS TWP.		6.625	8/ 1/95		6.45	HARRISBK
	500	BERNARDS TWP.		6.625	8/ 1/96		6.40	FIRWISC
	710	BERNARDS TWP.		6.625	8/ 1/97		6.50	FIRWISC

Figure 4.2 The Blue List of current municipal offerings (examples of pages). (Sample provided by Standard & Poor's, Blue List.)

```
120(EAST WINDSOR                      6.45    8/ 1/88        5.00)
 20(   (SER.)(GEN.IMP.)(W.I.)         6.45    8/ 1/89        5.40)SYN.4984
   (   DTD 8/1/86 F/C 2/1/87                                     )
```

```
MERRILNE    PRUBASYN    HUTTONNY    SMITHBSY    ROOSEVLT    TUCKERNY
THOMSON     COOGANGI    MOORESCH    POLLOCKW    MOSLYNY     MARINNYC
MOSLYPHL    OUTWATER
```

```
     50 EDISON TWP.            P/R @ 102    9.50   10/ 1/96 C91    6.00 DCNYMUN
    100 ESSEX CO.                           6.60    6/ 1/00        6.75 ADVESTPH
      5 EWING&LAWRENCE SWR.AU.              6.80   12/15/94         100 KIDDERSY
     30 GLOUCESTER CO.P.C.R. (MONSANTO)     7.25    7/ 1/05         100 ADVESTPH
+    25 GLOUCESTER TWP.BD.OF ED.            9.375  12/ 1/88        4.75 STOEVERG
    200 HACKENSACK                          6.50    8/ 1/88        4.80 MERRILNE
    140 HACKENSACK                          6.50    8/ 1/89        5.20 MERRILNE
     15 HACKENSACK                          6.50    8/ 1/94         100 AWDPHILA
     45 HANOVER TWP.SWR.AU.                 4.50   12/ 1/93        6.40 SMITHBRT
     30 HANOVER TWP.SWR.AU.                 4.50   12/ 1/94        6.60 SMITHBRT
     10 HANOVER TWP.SWR.AU.                 4.50   12/ 1/95        6.85 SMITHBRT
+    10 HOPEWELL TWP.        *REG* FGIC     7.375   7/ 1/01        7.10 GRUNTAL
    450 HOWELL TWP.                 MBIA    6.875   8/ 1/90        5.75 MANUFHAN
    350 HOWELL TWP.                         6.875   8/ 1/91        6.00 MANUFHAN
     35 HOWELL TWP.M.U.A.      CA @ 102     7.40    1/ 1/97 C96    7.20 GABRIELE
    165 HOWELL TWP.M.U.A.      CA @ 102     7.75    1/ 1/10 C96    7.50 GABRIELE
+   490 JERSEY CITY                         7.30    8/ 1/87        4.75 CHEMIC8K
     10 JERSEY CITY           STATE AID    5        6/ 1/88        5.00 SMITHBRT
```

```
   (JERSEY CITY                                                      )
490(   (HUDSON CO.)(SCH.BD.)(U.T.)        7.75    8/ 1/88        5.25)SYN.4453
   (   DTD 8/1/86 F/C 2/1/87                                         )
```

```
PRUBASYN    MERRILNY    HUTTONNY    SHEARNYA    SMITHBSY    ROOSEVLT
TUCKERP     DWRNY       THOMSON     BROWNCLA    COOGANGI    MOORESCH
MOOSEACO    PRINTKNJ    MARINNYC    ABROWNBA    OUTWATER    CFNBOFNJ
FBC         MOSLYNY     CAFFCERE    POLLOCKW    ADAMSMCE    LEBENTHA
ADVESTNY    RAMIREZ     CHEMIC8K    DREXELNY    KIDDERNY    FIKINTER
GRUNTAL     JBHANUER    UNDERHIL    MERRILNY
```

```
(D)  195 JERSEY CITY            SCH. QUAL.    7.75    8/ 1/89    *   5.70 COOGANGI
+     45 JERSEY CITY                          5.90   11/ 1/90        5.75 SMITHBRT
       5 JERSEY CITY            *REG* AMBAC   5.90    1/ 1/91         100 THOMSNSY
      50 JERSEY CITY                  AMBAC   6.45    1/ 1/94         101 ROOSEVLT
      90 JERSEY CITY            QUAL.WTR.     5.75   12/ 1/95        6.40 HALPERT
      85 JERSEY CITY            *REG* AMBAC   6.70    1/ 1/96         100 THOMSNSY
.     40 JERSEY CITY SWR.AU.          AMBAC   5.70    1/ 1/90         100 COOGANGI
      75 JERSEY CITY SWR.AU,          AMBAC   5.90    1/ 1/91         100 HALPERT
      75 JERSEY CITY SWR.AU,          AMBAC   6.45    1/ 1/94         100 COOGANGI
      50 JERSEY CITY SWR.AU.          AMBAC   6.45    1/ 1/94         100 WILLIAMA
      50 JERSEY CITY SWR.AU.          AMBAC   6.60    1/ 1/95         100 COOGANGI
     100 JERSEY CITY SWR.AU.          AMBAC   6.60    1/ 1/95         100 FIRMONSE
     100 JERSEY CITY SWR.AU.          AMBAC   6.60    1/ 1/95         100 WILLIAMA
      50 JERSEY CITY SWR.AU.          AMBAC   6.80    1/ 1/97         100 FIRMONSE
     100 JERSEY CITY SWR.AU.          AMBAC   6.80    1/ 1/97         100 WILLIAMA
+     90 JERSEY CITY SWR.AU.  W.I.    AMBAC  7        1/ 1/99         101 MOORESCH
     100 JERSEY CITY SWR.AU.          AMBAC   7.10    1/ 1/00         100 FIRMONSE
      25 JERSEY CITY SWR.AU.          AMBAC   7.10    1/ 1/00         100 MATTHEWS
     100 JERSEY CITY SWR.AU.          AMBAC   7.10    1/ 1/00         100 WILLIAMA
     100 JERSEY CITY SWR.AU.          AMBAC   7.25    1/ 1/06         100 FIRMONSE
+    250 JERSEY CITY SWR.AU.          AMBAC   7.25    1/ 1/14      100 1/2 BRISLINJ
+    150 JERSEY CITY SWR.AU.          AMBAC   7.25    1/ 1/14      100 1/2 FREEMAN
     100 JERSEY CITY SWR.AU.          AMBAC   7.25    1/ 1/14         100 FIRMONSE
```

```
   100(                                6.70    8/ 1/89        5.40)
+   70(LITTLE FERRY                    6.70    8/ 1/92        6.20)
    20(   DTD 8/1/86 F/C 2/1/87 W.I.   6.70    8/ 1/93        6.40)SYN.4917
    70(                                6.70    8/ 1/94        6.50)
    60(                                6.70    8/ 1/95        6.60)
```

49

The offering price of 89 is the price in theory at which this dealer would sell this particular bond on the day that this entry was placed in *The Blue List*. This price has nothing to do with the price at which Dillon, Read would *buy* the bond from you; that price would reflect the bid side of the market. The price of 89 also may be quite stale; unless the dealer takes action to change the price to reflect market movements, the price in *The Blue List* remains unchanged. The small star, labeled B, indicates that the price of this particular entry is a new price for that day's *The Blue List*; this price would be a better indicator of where these particular bonds are being offered by dealers because it was updated the day before.

Municipal bonds are offered by dealers to investors and to other dealers by two different pricing modes: dollar price and basis price. Dollar price is just that: so many dollars per bond. Dollar pricing is normally used for term bonds, which are larger quantities of bonds that were issued by the same municipality with the bonds having the same interest rate and maturity date. Most municipal bonds, however, are priced in basis price. Basis price indicates the yield that the investor will receive on the bond if the bond is held to maturity. Because the interest rate and maturity date are fixed when bonds are issued, basis pricing allows bonds with these two fixed characteristics to be priced to reflect changing market conditions.

The New Jersey Turnpike Authority bond issue, item A in Figure 4.2, is an example of a term bond priced in dollars; bonds priced in dollars are called "dollar bonds" in the municipal market.

For an example of a bond priced in basis, look at item C. Here we see $25,000 of Bergen County, New Jersey, bonds with an 8% coupon, maturing on June 1, 1993, offered to yield a return of 6.25 if the bonds are held to maturity. The 6.25 is the basis price. By the use of a bond calculator, this yield or basis price translates into a dollar price of approximately 109.41. If an investor purchased $10,000 par value of these bonds, the price would be $10,941 plus accrued interest. We will discuss the pricing mechanics of municipal bonds in detail in the chapter on Bond Math.

The " + " symbol, marked D, indicates that this is a new entry in its entirety; these bonds were not listed in the previous day's *The Blue List*. As with the indicator of a new price, the bonds listed as new entries are better guides to current market offerings and prices.

Let's return to the upper part of the left column. The entries marked E show five listings for the exact same bond, the New Jersey Turnpike 5.70% due May 1, 2013. Notice that five dealers are offering the identical bonds at five different prices ranging from a low of 86 to a high of 90. This translates to prices ranging from a low of $860 to a high of $900 for each $1000 par value of bonds. The question that you probably would ask is, "What is the correct price?" This question cannot be answered by looking at *The Blue List* because you now know that any price entered in *The Blue List* could be out of date. The only way to uncover the lowest price should you wish to purchase some of these bonds would be to call each of the five dealers and ask at what price they actually would offer to sell the bond in question. However, even if you were to do this, you might find that some of the dealers listed are no longer selling that particular bond issue. The listing of a bond in *The Blue List* does not always mean the bond is available. Be prepared to have a second choice if you are using *The Blue List*.

The lack of an efficient pricing mechanism in the municipal secondary market is one of the negative features of this market for the individual investor. The absence of a stock exchange or a NASDAQ screen puts you at a decided disadvantage when buying or selling tax-exempt bonds.

FLOATING SUPPLY OF BONDS

The Blue List totals the par value of all the bonds offered by dealers throughout the country each day. The bonds offered in the secondary market based on this summation has been ranging between $1.5 and $2.5 billion in recent years. Municipal bond dealers will not necessarily list all the bonds they have for sale in *The Blue List*, but *The Blue List* normally will contain a high percentage of them. Bonds available for sale and trading in the secondary market are called the floating supply. Even if the floating supply is several billion dollars of municipal bonds, the secondary market can be rather thin for dealer trading purposes. A dealer's trading activity is concentrated in larger lots of highly marketable bonds, whereas a large percentage of the floating supply shown in *The Blue List* consists of small lots of less marketable and less desirable bonds. This lack of supply of bonds with good trading characteristics can lead to increased market volatility and price fluctuation. If several larger municipal dealer trading firms decide to buy bonds for their inventories at the same time, the municipal market will rise in price by a greater amount than would be anticipated because the dealers all will be seeking the same general type of bonds for their inventory. In a similar fashion, the community of dealers trying to lessen their inventories during the same period drives prices down more than would be expected. The thinness of the floating supply and the resulting price volatility must be considered as another negative factor of the secondary market for municipal bonds.

SPREADS IN THE SECONDARY MARKET

If *The Blue List* is a guide to the offered side of the secondary market, what can we find out about the bid side of this market? How does the secondary market function when the investor needs a bid in order to sell some municipal bonds? A good way to approach these questions is to look at the spreads between the bid and offered side of the market as bonds trade in the secondary market. The spread is the difference between the price the dealer will pay for a bond and the price at which the dealer will offer the same bond for sale. The spread represents the dealer's profit potential in the transaction. It is in your interest if you are selling bonds in the secondary market to have as small a spread as possible associated with the bonds you are selling. A small spread means a better bid for the seller.

The spread is a function of many variables, including:

1. Number of bonds for sale: spreads will be greater for smaller lots of bonds. You will obtain a better bid if you are selling bonds in multiples of $25,000 par value. The best possible bid will be received on the sale of bonds in multiples of $100,000, as $100,000 constitutes a round lot. If you are selling less than a round lot, the spread will increase and the bid you receive will be lowered. An exception to $100,000 constituting a round lot can be made for dollar bonds. Because dollar bonds result from large bond issues with all the bonds having the same coupon rate and maturity, they are more actively traded than serial bonds, which have a much greater variety of coupons and maturities. For dollar bonds, a round lot of dollar bonds would be $25,000 par value as opposed to $100,000 par value. The largest spread—and poorest bid—will be associated with the sale of odd lots of bonds of less than $25,000 par value. Odd lot transactions never work to the investor's benefit. When you are purchasing municipal bonds, you do not obtain bonds at a lower price if you buy an odd lot of bonds; in fact, you may pay a higher price per bond because you are buying a small quantity of bonds. If you are selling an odd lot of bonds, you will always receive a lower price per bond for the securities you are selling. Odd lots of bonds have high unit transaction costs, which are reflected in higher offering prices when you are buying and in lower bids when you are selling.

2. Maturity of the bonds to be sold: the shorter the time to the maturity of the bond, the smaller the spread; the longer

the maturity, the greater the spread. This results from the higher risk associated with long-term bonds.

3. Bond quality: bonds of a higher quality with good bond ratings will have smaller spreads than will bonds with lower ratings.

4. Market conditions: the stronger the bond market when you are selling bonds, the smaller the spread. Dealers will be more aggressive in their bidding strategy if they think that the bond market is moving toward higher prices and lower yields for bonds. Correspondingly, depressed market conditions cause spreads to increase.

The more of these four factors in your favor when you are trying to sell bonds, the better the bids and the more money you receive for your bonds. However, if all four factors come up against the investor trying to sell bonds, the results will be very unfavorable. Trying to sell small, odd lots of long-term, poorly rated bonds in a declining market will never result in a favorable bid; in fact, in this situation there may not be any bid at all for your bonds.

FIGURING THE BID ON YOUR BONDS

Let's look at a more normal situation. If an investor has $25,000 par value of bonds to sell in a stable market, what is the difference between the bid and offered side of the market? Just what kinds of spreads will the investor face? Figure 4.3 gives you an indication of typical spreads for various maturities and bond qualities. If you are armed with some indication of the spread on a bond, you can determine what the approximate bid should be on your bonds by taking the following steps:

1. Obtain an offering from your bond dealer of matching or similar bonds to the bonds you are considering selling.

FIGURE 4.3. Municipal Bond Spreads in Points
(1 point equals $10.00 per $1,000 bond)

Bond Rating	Aaa	Aa	A	Baa
Short-term (approx. 1 yr)	¾	¾	1	1½
Intermediate-term (approx. 10 yr)	1	1	1½	2–3
Long-term (20 yr and longer)	1½–2	2	2½–3	3–4

2. Using Figure 4.3 find the approximate spread on the bond.

3. Subtract the spread from the offered price you received in step 1; this will give you an indication of what the approximate bid on your bonds should be.

Here's an example: You want to sell a block of $25,000 of an "A" rated bond with approximately 10 years to go to the bond's maturity. Your bond dealer offers you a bond of similar quality, coupon, and maturity at a price of 96. Looking at Figure 4.3, the spread on this type of bond would be about 1.5 points. Therefore, the bid on the bonds you want to sell should be approximately 94.5.

If you think that this is circuitous, you are absolutely right. But if you are going to be selling securities into an over-the-counter market that doesn't publish much information about price levels, you had better have some idea of what the bid might be or else you may be taken to the cleaners. Never forget the mottos of the municipal secondary market: "Let the buyer beware" and "What the market will bear."

Investors should always be aware that whenever they buy a municipal bond in the secondary market, they are buying the bond from the dealer who actually owns the bond. The buyer is not purchasing the bond from an investor who is selling the bond in question. In a similar fashion, when you sell a bond, you are selling the bond to a dealer. The bid that the dealer makes is just that—the dealer's bid. The bid may, or may not, be an honest bid; it may, or may not, reflect market conditions. Unfortunately, investors can find themselves selling bonds at an auction with their bond dealer being the only bidder present at the auction. Obviously, this is a tough way to get a good price on the bonds you are selling.

If you are selling municipal bonds, get bids from more than one dealer. You will be pleasantly surprised at the differences in bids you can receive on the exact same bonds from various dealers. Most investors have access to several municipal bond dealers because most major stock brokerage firms and commercial banks are dealers in tax-exempt securities, and the typical investor may have account relationships with more than one of these financial organizations. Shop around and you will find that you will get more money for the bonds you are selling: it only takes a few phone calls.

USING THE NEWSPAPERS

There is one small glimmer of light in the tunnel of the secondary market for the investor trying to obtain price information about bonds. *The Wall Street Journal* and other major newspapers publish a table with bid information about tax-exempt bonds. A sample is shown in Figure 4.4. However, this table is deficient for two reasons: first, the table only shows 40 municipal bonds. Forty bonds is a poor sample when we consider how many different types of municipal bonds have been issued and are still "alive and ticking." There are millions of different combinations and permutations of outstanding municipal bonds. Showing 40 issues would compare with the newspapers listing only IBM stock to show what is happening on the New York Stock Exchange. Secondly, the data represent bids for large

TAX-EXEMPT BONDS

Friday, June 06, 1986

Here are representative current prices for several active tax-exempt revenue and refunding bonds, based on large institutional trades. Changes are rounded to the nearest one-eighth. Yield is to maturity.

Issue	Coupon	Mat.	Price	Chg.	Yld.
Austin Tx Comb Ut Sys86A	8.000	11-15-16	91¾	...	8.78
Cal Pub Wk Bd Lease	7.375	11-01-05	93½	+ ⅛	8.03
Cal Poll Cont Au PacG&E	7.500	05-01-16	94⅛	+ ¼	8.02
Cape May Ut NJ Sewer	7.250	01-01-16	91½	+ ½	8.01
Chgo O'Hare Airport	8.750	01-01-16	101¾	+ ¼	8.58
Chgo School Fin Au Ser86	7.750	06-01-09	92	+ ¼	8.55
Chgo School Fin Au Ser86	7.700	06-01-06	91¾	+ ¼	8.56
D of C G.O. Ref Ser86A	7.875	06-01-06	94⅞	+ ⅞	8.40
E Bay Mud Cal W 86	7.000	03-01-08	91	+ ⅛	7.87
Fla Bd of Ed Ser86A	7.800	06-01-17	97½	...	8.02
Fla Muni Pwr St Lucie86	7.375	10-01-16	87⅛	+ ¼	8.57
Fla Muni Pwr St Lucie86	7.125	10-01-13	89⅛	+ ⅛	8.11
Ga Muni El Au Gn Pw	7.875	01-01-18	91⅜	+ ⅝	8.68
HoustonWtr Prior Lien Rev	8.200	12-01-16	97	+ ½	8.47
Interm'tn Pw Sup Utah	7.750	07-01-17	91⅞	+ ⅝	8.50
Interm'tn Ser H&I	9.000	07-01-19	103⅛	+ 1⅛	8.70
Jacksonvile El St John	7.250	10-01-09	91⅛	+ ⅜	8.10
Jacksonvile El St John	7.500	10-01-14	90⅝	+ ½	8.39
Met Seattle Sew Ser P	7.400	01-01-16	89½	+ ⅛	8.36
Mich Pub Pw Bell River	7.250	01-01-12	90⅜	+ ¼	8.15
Muni Asst Cp NYC Ser 57	7.250	07-01-08	92	+ ⅝	8.02
NC East Muni Pow Ag	7.750	01-01-15	89⅝	+ ⅜	8.77
NJ Highway Garden St Pk	7.125	01-01-14	89⅛	+ ⅛	8.11
NYC Muni Cp Ser 58	7.375	07-01-08	93⅛	+ ⅝	8.04
NYS Dorm NYS Ser85 A&B	8.500	07-01-15	104⅜	+ ¼	8.11
NYS Pwr Auth Series T	7.375	01-01-18	93⅝	+ ¼	7.92
NYS Pwr Auth Series T	7.300	01-01-10	94⅞	+ ½	7.78
P Rico Hous AG Sing-Fam	7.500	12-01-15	92¾	...	8.15
Platte Riv El Rev Ser 1	7.700	06-01-16	94½	+ ¼	8.20
Riverside Ca El 86A	7.000	10-01-13	88⅝	+ ¼	8.03
Salt River Ariz El Sys	7.000	01-01-17	86¼	+ ¼	8.24
San Antonio Prior Lien86	7.250	05-01-12	87⅞	+ ¼	8.40
SCal Pub Pwr Tr Pro SerB	7.375	07-01-21	90½	+ ½	8.21
SCal Pub Pwr Tr	7.875	07-01-18	95½	+ ⅜	8.28
So Cent Conn Reg Wat	7.125	08-01-12	90⅛	+ ¼	8.03
So Cent Conn Reg Wat	7.125	08-01-06	90⅛	+ ¼	8.12
Springfield Ill El Jr Lien	7.750	03-01-06	94⅛	+ ⅛	8.36
Univ Mich Reg Hosp	7.750	12-01-12	93⅝	+ ⅜	8.35
Wash St G.O.	8.000	09-01-09	97⅝	+ ½	8.23
Wash St G.O.	8.000	09-01-05	97⅝	+ ½	8.25

Source: The Bond Buyer, New York.

Figure 4.4 Tax-exempt bonds. (Reprinted by permission of *The Wall Street Journal,* © Dow Jones & Company, Inc., 1986. All rights reserved.)

blocks of bonds. A bid is the price a dealer is willing to pay for a bond if the bond is offered for sale. You can expect to pay more than the bid prices shown in the table if you are a buyer of bonds. If you are purchasing \$25,000 of any of the bonds in Figure 4.4, you can expect to pay two to three points, or \$20 to \$30 per \$1000 par value, more than the prices shown in Figure 4.4.

Don't make the mistake of investing in one of the bonds solely because it is listed on this table. The bonds on the table are constantly being changed to show newly issued bonds in the primary market. The only value of this table is to show market direction and price changes on a day-to-day basis.

ENTER THE BROKERS

There is another important group of players in the secondary market for tax-exempt bonds. They are the municipal bond brokers. In the municipal market, dealers are those individuals, companies, firms, or banks who underwrite, trade, and distribute bonds. Dealers have a position in the market; they own bonds in inventory and try to sell their bonds for a profit. There are hundreds of municipal bond dealers located throughout the country. There are, however, only approximately a dozen municipal bond brokers who are mostly located in New York City. Brokers have trading transactions only between dealers; brokers do not have any transactions directly with investors. If dealer A wants to buy or sell bonds to other dealers, dealer A can use a broker to assist in making the purchase or sale. Dealers use brokers to execute their buy and sell transactions in a short period; dealers also use brokers if the dealers wish to keep their buying or selling activities secret from competing dealers. For example, if dealer A wants to increase his municipal position without other dealers being aware of his strategy, dealer A will use a broker so that other dealers will not know that it is dealer A who is accumulating inventory. By providing a variety of services to dealers, brokers make an important contribution to the overall liquidity of the municipal market.

If you are aware of these brokers, you can use them to your advantage when you want to sell municipal bonds. Rather than taking your bonds to a dealer for just one bid, smart investors will ask their dealer to have the bonds sold through a municipal bond broker.

The larger brokers have telex wire services linking the various dealers. One dealer "gives" the bonds to a broker; the broker "shows" or displays the bonds on a telex to hundreds of dealers all over the country. Interested dealers bid on the bonds directly to the broker, and the broker relays the highest bid to the dealer who initiated the transaction. Obviously, it is better to get many bids rather than one bid for your bonds when you are trying to sell them; the more bids the merrier. Ask your dealer if the dealership will accommodate a sale of bonds for you by this method. If the dealer is not interested in this procedure, maybe it's time to change your dealer. Be aware that the dealer will charge you for this service. The fee should be between $2.50 and $5.00 per $1000 bond for most transactions of this nature. This method of selling bonds is especially helpful if the investor is selling a number of different bonds from different states and municipalities. No one dealer will have the best bid on each lot of bonds on a diversified list of bonds for sale. You must advertise a transaction of this nature to many dealers—and the broker's market is the only efficient way to accomplish this task.

YET IT WORKS

Despite the faults and weaknesses of the secondary market for municipal bonds when compared with the secondary markets for other types of securities, this market functions with sufficient efficiency to provide the liquidity that is needed by investors. Each year, the secondary market trades a volume of municipal bonds estimated at twice the volume in the new issue market; this means that approximately $400 billion dollars worth of bonds were traded in the municipal over-the-counter secondary market in 1985. However, the investor should be aware that this market is very different from the type of market provided by a stock exchange. The buyer or seller of municipal bonds who approaches the secondary market aware of the factors that have been discussed in this chapter will be in a better position to obtain a more favorable price on the purchase or sale of municipal bonds.

POINTS TO REMEMBER

1. The secondary market for municipals is not as efficient as other secondary markets for securities.
2. If you know how to use it, *The Blue List* can be a helpful tool.
3. Try to get an indication of the reasonableness and competitiveness of the price of a bond being offered to you before making the purchase.
4. Try to construct an estimate of what the bid will be on the municipal bonds you are trying to sell before soliciting any bids.
5. Get bids from several dealers or use a bond broker.
6. Be careful and let "caveat emptor" be your motto.

5

general

obligation bonds

Municipal securities have traditionally been divided into two major categories: general obligation bonds and revenue bonds. The division is based on the method by which the issuing state or municipality raises the money to pay the interest and principal due the bond holder.

General obligation bonds are backed by the taxing power of the issuer. The primary tax levy used by municipalities is the property tax. On the state level, income, business, and sales taxes, and various fees typically are pledged to repay debt obligations. Revenue bonds, which will be the topic of the next chapter, are serviced by user fees. As you can imagine, the world of municipal bonds is not one of a clean and simple division into either the general obligation or the revenue category. Many bond issues fall into a gray area between these two categories; these issues have some characteristics of both types of bonds, and it is sometimes difficult for individual investors to determine if they have invested in a general obligation or a revenue bond.

General obligation bonds are issued to provide the capital needed to build structures and improvements that will be used by the entire community. Examples of items financed by general obligation bonds include governmental offices, public schools, and roads and bridges that do not impose toll charges. In addition to paying for these types of capital structures, general obligation bonds would be used to buy items such as office and school equipment, police cars, and computer systems. In theory, a municipality undertakes these expenditures to provide services for the general community. In theory, everyone in the community benefits from the services that result from the sale of general obligation bonds, and therefore, everyone is taxed to help pay the debt service on the bonds.

There are three characteristics that distinguish general obligation bonds from revenue bonds. First, general obligations are normally approved by the voters at a general or special election. Voter authorization for bonds ranges from a simple vote on a school bond issue to a complex change in a state's constitution allowing expanded state borrowing. Second, nearly everyone in the community will be taxed to raise the money needed for debt service. Users and nonusers alike will have to pay to finance the facility that benefits the community. Third, the money raised for debt service will be based on property values or income levels. There will be no direct correlation between the value received by an individual member of the community from the facility being financed and the amount an individual must contribute to pay the interest and principal on the bonds. The more affluent members of the community will bear a heavier cost than the less affluent.

TYPES OF GENERAL OBLIGATION BONDS

Although all general obligation bonds are supported by taxing power, there are various types of general obligation bonds.

The *unlimited tax* bond is the classic example of the general obligation bond. The majority of general obligation bonds issued by states and municipalities are unlimited tax bonds. Unlimited tax general obligation bonds represent the most secure class of tax-exempt securities. These bonds are backed by the imposition of taxes on all taxable property in a community. There is no limit as to the rate of taxation that can be applied to the property being taxed to raise funds for debt service on the bonds. These securities have the strength of unlimited taxing power on real property that cannot be moved or hidden from the tax collector. Because states normally do not impose property taxes, a general obligation bond of a state would be backed by the state's total taxing power and the pledge of its full faith and credit.

Limited tax bonds are general obligation bonds that have restrictions as to the amount of taxes that can be raised for debt service. For example, a limited tax bond would result if there is a maximum rate of property taxation that can be levied by a community. Tax limits may be found either hidden in state or local finance laws or may have been incorporated into the bond authorization approved by the voters. Whenever you invest in a general obligation bond, you should know if there are any limitations on taxes that could be imposed to raise the funds needed to pay off the bonds. Ask the bond dealer who is selling you the bond if it is a limited tax bond, and if tax levying restrictions do exist, weigh these restrictions as part of the investment decision.

A *double-barreled* bond has the characteristics of both a general obligation bond and a revenue bond. Typically this bond is paid in the first instance from fees charged for using a facility or service, but if the fees fall short of the amount needed for principal and interest payments, then the taxing power of the state or municipality would be used to cover the shortfall. This type of bond is often found in financing water and sewer systems: fees are charged the users of the system, and property taxes will be used if the fees collected do not provide sufficient receipts to cover operating and financial costs. The double-barreled bond has the obvious advantage of having two potential sources of payment, and extra sources of payment means extra security for the bondholder.

Three types of bonds that are found in the gray area between general obligations and revenues are lease obligations, moral obligations, and certificates of participation. I consider these types of bonds closer to general obligations than to revenue bonds because the ultimate source of backing is the taxing power of the issuing state or municipality. However, these bonds normally do not have voter approval, and their claim to the taxing power of the issuing community can be indirect and may be subject to annual authorization by a legislative body.

A *lease obligation* bond's principal and interest is paid from lease payments made by a municipality to an authority that constructs and rents a facility to the municipality. For example, in Pennsylvania, many public schools and municipal buildings are constructed by the sale of the bonds issued by a local authority.

After the authority constructs the building, it is rented on a long-term lease to the local school district or community, and the lease payments provide the funds for the debt service for the authority's bonds. These bonds appear to be revenue bonds on the surface, but because the school district or local community is using its general taxing powers to raise the funds for the lease payments, lease obligations are closer to general obligation bonds than to revenues.

The *moral obligation* bond is another bond found somewhere between the general obligation bond and the revenue bond. When a moral obligation bond is sold—usually by a state authority—included in the money raised in the initial bond sale will be sufficient funds to establish a debt reserve fund. This fund will have enough money to pay the highest debt service that will occur in any year that the bonds are outstanding. Debt service is the amount of money needed in any given year to pay interest, principal repayments for maturing bonds, and sinking fund requirements that may exist for the bonds. The word "reserve" is the key word in "debt reserve fund." The debt reserve fund will only be drawn upon if the issuing authority has a shortfall in its normal income stream and does not have sufficient money to meet its principal or interest requirements. When the reserve fund is drawn upon, the state must appropriate money to replenish it. The money that is used to replenish the fund will come from the state's general taxing power. For this reason, the moral obligation bond resembles a general obligation bond more than a revenue bond. An appropriation of money by a state to replenish the fund typically is subject to approval by the state legislature. There are no cases to my knowledge where a state legislature has failed to appropriate money to maintain an authority's debt reserve fund. It is highly unlikely that a state would not appropriate the funds to support a moral obligation bond because there would be severe adverse financial repercussions resulting from the failure of a state to replenish the debt reserve fund. The bond market would exact a penalty in the form of higher interest costs for future borrowings, not only by the state in question, but by municipalities located in the state. This penalty would surely be more costly over time than whatever state money would be needed to support moral obligation debt. For this reason, I recommend that you consider these bonds for your portfolio. The fact that a bond has a moral obligation reserve fund is found in the bond's official statement. Your bond dealer will be able to assist you in finding these bonds in the marketplace. The return on any state's moral obligation bonds will be higher than the return on the general obligation bonds of the same state. Take the extra return; the extra risk is minimal.

Certificates of participation constitute the third type of bond found between general obligations and revenues. The use of certificates of participation by states and municipalities has been growing in recent years. Municipalities on occasion purchase equipment that will be financed by an installment sales contract. The certificate of participation represents an investor's interest in the payments of the installment sales agreement. Certificates of participation have all the tax advantages that characterize municipal bonds. Their ultimate financial backing is the ability of the state or municipality to make the contractual lease payments; additionally, they can be secured by the assets being purchased. Certificates of participation can yield about 50 to 100 basis points more than general obligation bonds of the same municipality. However, certificates of participation have a poor secondary market and therefore are less liquid than general obligation bonds. This is not a great problem for most investors, because the maturity for these types of tax-exempt investments usually is in the two- to 10-year range. Should you invest in these instruments, you would be well advised to plan on holding the certificates to maturity. Certificates of participation should be considered by municipal investors if their quality, maturity, and return are attractive; however, because of their illiquidity, they should not form more than approximately 20% of an individual investor's municipal portfolio.

SOURCES OF INFORMATION

Where do you obtain information about general obligation bonds? The primary source is the issuing state or municipality itself through its official statement. As we saw in Chapter 2, when a bond issue is sold, an official statement will be prepared describing the issue and the municipality. The official statement is a booklet of detailed and technical information anywhere from 25 to more than 100 pages in length. For the average investor, the official statement contains more information than is needed to make an investment decision. This document is used mainly by professional municipal bond underwriters and analysts in reviewing and rating bonds.

Major dealers in municipal bonds produce research reports on general obligation bonds. These reports will be a few pages in length and will highlight and summarize the more detailed official statement. You must be warned about these reports, however, because many times the research report will present a rosy picture of a bond issue that the dealer is trying to sell. What looks like an unbiased research report can turn out to be a slick advertisement for a bond issue that the dealer is touting.

Probably the best source of readily available and useful information for the individual investor is the major rating agencies. Moody's and Standard & Poor's rate municipal bonds and provide information about bond issues for the investor. Most libraries have copies of *Moody's Municipal & Government Manuals* in their reference section. These manuals provide information about states and municipalities that issue securities, details about the outstanding bonds, and ratings assigned to tax-exempt bonds. Larger libraries also may subscribe to municipal research reports issued by both Moody's and Standard & Poor's. The rating agencies do not have any interest in selling a particular security; as such, their reports and ratings are independent and free of bias that may be found in the reports issued by bond dealers.

ANALYZING AND RATING GENERAL OBLIGATION BONDS

As an investor, you should be aware of some of the major factors that are considered in analyzing and rating bonds. With some appreciation of the work of the bond analyst, the resulting bond rating becomes a more meaningful investment tool for you to use.

Always remember that the most you can expect from the typical bond investment will be the receipt of your interest payments when due and your principal at maturity. Most municipal bond investors that I know would be very satisfied if this could be absolutely guaranteed. By way of contrast, investing in equities always has the possibility of capital appreciation if the price of the stock rises. Because the amount of your "winnings" in the bond market is always fixed by the maturity value of the bonds, the bond analyst's task is to search for those factors that may prevent the expected receipt of interest and return of principal when due. Therefore, municipal bond analysts approach their tasks with a negative bias: looking for problems that can develop in the future more so than looking for strengths. The goal of the stock analyst on the other hand is to ferret out those positive investment situations with capital growth possibilities in the future.

Municipal bond analysis begins by studying various ratios.

Ratios of indebtedness to wealth, debt per capita, percentage of uncollected taxes, and short-term debt to long-term indebtedness are some of the ratios developed by the bond analyst. These ratios are compared with the same community over time and with other communities.

A study also will be made of trends, to see what positive or negative changes are taking place in a municipality. The analyst will review changes in population, personal income, property values, indebtedness, and employment. Trends, like ratios, will be used as comparison data with other states and municipalities.

As general obligation bonds are paid by taxes, the analyst must look at the taxpayers and the economic base of the community. Is the tax base residential or industrial? If industrial property taxes are important in the tax base, what are the types of business activity? A base of diversified, quality business activities is more desirable than one of used car lots and junk yards.

These factors just highlight the work than an analyst undertakes in rating a general obligation bond. The key questions for you to remember are: first, what is the value of a rating for me, and second, how good are bond ratings?

A bond rating is a crutch for the investor. It is good to lean on the rating, but don't rest all your investment decision on it. Times and conditions change, and sometimes the changes occur so rapidly that the bond rating is valueless.

A recent example of how rapidly ratings can change can be seen in the defaulted bonds of the Washington Public Power Supply System #4 and #5. Although this issue is a revenue bond, it demonstrates just how fast ratings can change on any type of municipal bond. An investor buying this bond in early 1981 would have purchased a bond rated "A1" by Moody's; the "A1" rating would be a source of comfort to most investors. About two years later, however, the rating had dropped to "Caa" reflecting either actual default or a high risk of default. Rating changes like these occurring within approximately a two-year period are difficult for many investors to comprehend, especially when you consider that the bonds in question had maturities of up to 40 years. Remember that ratings are more analogous to opinions than to scientific findings.

Another factor you should consider when investing in general obligation bonds is whether or not to invest in a general obligation bond that is rated "Aaa." The "Aaa" rated bond can only go one way in the rating scheme, and that is down. If a bond is downgraded by the rating agency, the market value drops. Thus, the odds are definitely against you as downgrades from "Aaa" to a lower rating are more numerous than the occasional upgrades to "Aaa" from a lower rating. This statement does not apply to investing in "Aaa" insured bonds; these bonds will be discussed in Chapter 11.

SPECIAL INVESTING SITUATIONS

When investing in general obligations, consider the special situation that exists with the general obligations of any of the 50 states. Defaults and problems have occurred in recent years with general obligation bonds of municipalities: New York City and Cleveland are two examples. However, a default on the part of a state is a highly unlikely event. Defaults by municipalities are partially financial (there isn't enough money in the till) and partially political (a larger political body refuses to provide assistance). If one of the states were in financial difficulty, the federal government would probably support the state and prevent a default rather than run the risk of unfavorable international financial repercussions that could result from a state's default. Look for state general obligation bonds with lower ratings accompanied by higher returns. Look for general obligation bonds issued by those states that might find themselves in a temporary financial bind.

Another class of bonds that deserve special consideration by investors is the moral obligation bonds we have already discussed. Moral obligation bonds represent excellent value, and in many cases, are undervalued by the marketplace and by bond investors.

Whenever you invest in general obligations, keep in mind that the larger the geographic area backing the bond, the better the investment. All other things being equal, a county bond is safer than a town bond, and a state bond is safer than a county bond. Because taxes are the basis for the payment of debt service, the larger and more diversified the area to be taxed, the better the credit of the bond.

A final strong category of general obligations is school bonds. Today a large percentage of the revenues of many school districts comes from state aid payments. A relatively weak, "Baa" rated, school district located in a higher rated state can represent an excellent investment opportunity if state aid payments form an important part of the total revenue stream of the school district.

Look for other situations in which states and counties protect the financial viability of school districts. In New York State, for example, if there is a delinquency in the collection of school district property taxes, the county in which the school district is located must advance funds to the school district to cover the delinquency; furthermore, the collection of the delinquent taxes becomes the responsibility of the county, not the school district. This requirement of a county guaranteeing the school district's tax collections obviously makes a weak school district located in a financially strong county a much better investment than would be indicated by the rating on the bonds of the school district itself. There are some exceptions to this rule in New York State; city school districts, including New York City, and school districts located in Westchester County are not protected by this county guarantee of tax collections.

SOME FINAL THOUGHTS ABOUT GENERAL OBLIGATIONS

Before you invest in a general obligation bond, ask yourself the following questions:

1. What is the rating? Make sure the rating meets your investment objectives. Never invest in a nonrated bond. Most nonrated bonds are speculations, not investments. Most municipal bond investors will find that "A" rated bonds probably represent the best overall investment.

2. Where is the community issuing the bonds? If you don't know where a community is located, how can you possibly invest in its bonds? This point seems so basic and simple, yet I have come across many situations in which investors own a municipal bond and they have no idea where the issuing community is located! Incredible, but true.

3. Am I familiar with the community? If you are willing to invest money in the bonds of a community, be willing to invest some time in learning about the community. This is the best advice I can give the investor buying general obligation bonds. Most investors can purchase bonds issued by their own or surrounding communities, or issued by communities the investors may have visited on business or vacation. Three important words to remember when investing in general obligation bonds are: "Know the issuer."

4. But aren't all general obligations super safe investments? Don't ever rest on the old adage that the general obligation bondholder gets paid interest and principal before all other

expenditures of the state or municipality. Just because a bond is a general obligation, don't assume it is a safe investment. If the municipality gets into financial trouble, and push comes to shove, it will be the bondholder who gets pushed and shoved early on in the game.

6

revenue bonds

Revenue bonds are backed solely by specific, well-defined, and limited sources of income. These bonds are not secured by the general taxing power of the issuer as are general obligation bonds. Many times an investor sees the name of a particular state or municipality as part of the title of a revenue bond and erroneously concludes that the obligation has the backing of the state or municipality in question. This is not so. The funds that are used to pay the holder of the revenue bonds are derived solely from the income received from the project being financed. If the project does not generate sufficient revenue to pay principal and interest, the bonds go into default. Because the source of repayment is limited, you must be especially knowledgeable about the project or facility being financed by the bonds before making an investment.

Revenue bonds have been on the investment scene for more than 100 years. The canals and turnpikes of 19th Century America were financed in part by revenue bond sales, and their modern day counterparts—our expressways and airports—also look to the municipal bond market to raise capital for construction and improvements.

The first issue that resembled today's revenue bond was sold by Spokane, Washington in 1897; this issue was backed solely by the revenues of the town's water system. Revenue bond issues have mushroomed in recent years. Figure 6.1 shows the growth of revenue bonds during the past 20 years. In additional to this remarkable absolute growth of revenue bonds is the relative increase in revenue bond financing versus the relative decline in the sales of general obligation bonds. As shown in Figure 3.1, revenue bonds are becoming the more important component in the sale of newly issued state and municipal debt.

Facilities of all types have been financed by the sale of revenue bonds. There are the well-known bonds that are backed by revenues received from water, sewer, and electric systems; toll bridges and tunnels; and housing projects. But on rare occasions,

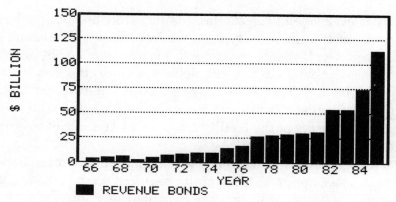

Figure 6.1   Revenue bonds (Courtesy *The Bond Buyer*.)

revenue bonds have even financed such exotic activities as race tracks, liquor stores, and massage parlors. Revenue bonds have been issued for almost every conceivable purpose as long as there hopefully will be a stream of income to cover the principal and interest requirements of the bonds.

WHY REVENUE BONDS ARE ISSUED

There are four major reasons why states and municipalities issue revenue bonds rather than general obligations: 1) the question of equity, 2) avoidance of voter approval, 3) constitutional restrictions prohibiting general obligation bond sales, and 4) holding general obligation bond sales in reserve for the future.

Revenue bonds can be considered to be more equitable to the community's taxpayers than general obligations. Revenue bonds are backed by the fees that individuals or corporations pay for the use of some facility or service. If someone chooses not to use a particular service, or to use less of it than a neighbor, there will be less of a charge to that particular individual.

Whereas everyone in the community pays for the public school, everyone in the community does *not* have to use a toll road or bridge equally. If you do not use a toll bridge, you do not have to pay any fees that help pay the debt service on the bonds that built the bridge. This "user pays doctrine" of revenue bonds charges the cost of a facility or service more directly to the beneficiaries and users of the facility financed by the sale of revenue bonds.

As we discussed in Chapter 5, when general obligation bonds are sold, voter approval is normally required as the community in total will be taxed to pay the principal and interest on the bonds. Obviously, not all bonds that are placed on the ballot are approved by voters. Negative voter reaction to the possibility of higher taxes spells the demise of many bond authorizations on election day. Revenue bonds typically are issued without voter approval. A less than popular project can be financed by the sale of revenue bonds; the same project might be rejected if voters had to approve the sale of general obligation bonds to finance it.

There are cases in which a state or municipality has legal or constitutional restrictions on the amount of general obligation bonds that can be outstanding at any time. The only practical way around these restrictions is the sale of revenue bonds. For example, until a few years ago, the state of Georgia could not have more than $1 million general obligation bonds outstanding at any one time. Obviously, $1 million doesn't go very far today when we think of the nature and costs of the projects financed by municipal bonds. To circumvent this situation, Georgia sold revenue bonds through a variety of state authorities to meet the financial needs of the state.

A less stringent but more common restriction on general obligation bond sales is a limitation on the total amount of general obligation bonds outstanding to some realistic and workable amount. In this case if revenue bonds can be sold, the municipality keeps its general obligation borrowing authorization for future needs.

TERM BONDS: A SPECIAL CHARACTERISTIC OF REVENUE BONDS

Many revenue bonds are issued as term bonds. A term bond is one with a large number of bonds maturing on the same date and bearing the same rate of interest. From the investor's viewpoint, all the term bonds of one issue are identical and interchangeable just as each share of the common stock of a company is identitical and interchangeable. Term bonds are often referred to as "dollar bonds," because they are bought and sold in the secondary market in dollar prices as opposed to yield or basis prices.

Term bonds have two special positive characteristics for the individual investor. First, these bonds allow a purchaser to build a position in one bond over an extended period. Second, term bonds often have sinking funds.

As the initial issue of term bonds tends to be very large, these bonds are often available in the secondary market long after the initial sale. An investor who holds term bonds can usually purchase matching bonds if additional investments are made. It is difficult to purchase general obligation bonds to match the general obligation bonds you already might be holding, because general obligation bonds are sold as serial bonds with varying maturities. For example, consider two investors who each buy $25,000 worth of municipal bonds each year. Investor A purchases four different lots of bonds during a four-year period; no round lot of $100,000 par value of bonds is formed, and A must be concerned with the record keeping and interest collection for four separate issues. If A has to sell bonds in the secondary market, A finds that the bids on odd lots of bonds is lower than would be the case on a round lot. Investor B on the other hand understands the value of investing in term bonds. B also buys $25,000 worth of bonds at the same four times and in the same market conditions as does A. But B buys four lots of $25,000 of the same term bond issue. After the four transactions, B has one round lot of $100,000 par value of bonds, easier record keeping, simpler interest collection, and most importantly, a more marketable, more liquid bond portfolio.

A term bond normally has a sinking fund requirement. A sinking fund is a mandatory schedule of bonds that must be retired each year from the total number of term bonds still outstanding. The bonds will be retired either by the issuer purchasing bonds in the secondary market or by calling bonds on the basis of random numbers. The presence of a sinking fund, especially a sinking fund that is currently acting to retire bonds, is important because the retirement of bonds from a term issue supports the price of the remaining outstanding bonds in the secondary market.

The requirement to purchase bonds for sinking fund purposes adds another positive investment feature to some term bonds. There are several bond issues for which the municipality must call bonds for the sinking fund at par or 100. The issuer is restricted from purchasing bonds in the secondary market to meet the sinking fund requirements. If you can buy these bonds at a discount from par, you have the opportunity of making an attractive capital gains profit if the bonds you hold are called at par; of course, the capital gains profit would be in addition to the tax-exempt interest income you receive as long as you hold the bonds. For example, the sinking fund for the Massachusetts Port Authority, 5⅞% bonds, due July 1, 2012, calls bonds each July 1st at 100. Some bonds of this issue will be called each July until the final maturity of the issue. Because of the relatively low coupon, this issue has been selling in the secondary market at a discount. If you buy this bond at a price of 90, you will receive a 10 point gain, or $100 per $1000 bond, if any bonds you hold are called. Even though this bond has a final maturity of 2012, the average life of the bond issue will be much shorter because bonds are called and retired each year by the sinking fund. The operation on the sinking fund will result in an average maturity of the bond issue occurring in the year 2001, as opposed to the final stated maturity of 2012.

In addition to the Massachusetts Port Authority bond issue, there are three other term issues currently selling at discounts, whose sinking fund requirements must be purchased by calling bonds at par:

Kentucky Turnpike Authority, 5⅞%, 7/1/08
New Jersey Highway Authority, 6½%, 1/1/11
New Jersey Turnpike Authority, 5.7%, 5/1/13

The Massachusetts Port Authority issue and the three issues listed above have been prerefunded; that is, the issuing authority has already deposited with the paying agent the funds needed to pay the bonds principal and interest. As these bond issues are prerefunded, they have no credit risk and are rated "Aaa" by Moody's.

INVESTMENT FEATURES OF REVENUE BONDS

Analyzing revenue bonds in many ways is easier than analyzing general obligation bonds, because you are looking at specific sources of income. This is especially important as there are more potential pitfalls in investing in revenue bonds than there are in general obligations.

The first consideration should be the state of the project. Is the facility backing the bonds actually constructed and producing income? In this case, look at the track record to date. Is the facility under construction? Here we can examine the current state of the project: is it on time, close to budget, and without community opposition? Does the project exist only on paper? In this case, you are investing in a feasibility study.

Let's look at the following types of revenue bonds and analyze some of their positive and negative investment features: (1) electric power systems, (2) water and sewer systems, (3) transportation-related systems, (4) colleges and universities, (5) housing-related systems, (6) hospitals, (7) waste disposal systems, and (8) industrial development bonds.

ELECTRIC REVENUE BONDS

Revenue bonds backed by power systems represent the largest share of revenue bonds. Because of the nature of the systems being financed, these bonds tend to be very long-term investments.

There are negative features to both existing power systems and new construction. The existing systems tend to have older electric production and distribution facilities that can require substantial capital investment simply for basic maintenance. Newer systems have numerous potential problems for the municipal bond investor. In many cases, a new system issues revenue bonds years before any power is generated and any income is received. During the early years interest payments on the bonds come from funds received by selling additional bonds at the time of the initial financing. While the system is being constructed, many factors can develop causing extensive time delays and cost overruns that can result in serious problems for the bondholders. This is especially common with nuclear projects. The technology of nuclear power plant construction is always in a state of change, and the technological changes can result in severe financial problems. Tax-exempt bonds backed by unfinished nuclear power plants are for speculators, not for investors.

The two primary advantages of power revenue bonds are: power plants supply an economic commodity that is necessary for modern residential and industrial society, and the power supplier is normally in a semimonopolistic position with little or no competition. These advantages are balanced by the problems of high costs, increasing regulation from various levels of government, and environmental issues.

If you invest in power bonds, look for bonds of existing, constructed systems. Try to find systems where hydro or coal form the base for power production. Avoid systems that are heavily dependent on nuclear power, especially uncompleted nuclear power plants. Also avoid systems that are just starting to build their plants.

WATER AND SEWER REVENUE BONDS

Water and sewer revenue bonds generally represent excellent investments for the individual investor. These bonds are backed by the charges levied for water and sewerage services that are supplied by the issuing authority both to residences and businesses in a community. Obviously these are vital services for any community. What would happen if your water or sewerage charges were increased substantially? You really have no choice but to pay the increased fees. The monopolistic position of the authority, plus the vital nature of the services, combine to make these bonds very safe and secure.

However, the investor should consider the community being serviced before investing in water and sewer revenues. In this respect, these bonds should be analyzed as if they were general obligations. The revenues to support water and sewer revenue bonds are derived from a limited geographic area, and the investor should be aware of the economic characteristics of the serviced area. Any "A" rated water and sewer revenue bond that is providing service to a community whose general obligation bonds are also rated "A" would be well recommended.

TRANSPORTATION REVENUE BONDS

Transportation-related bonds are backed by user fees. When you pay a toll to use a highway, cross a bridge, or enter a tunnel, part of that toll may be going to pay the principal and interest for the municipal bonds that financed the facility. Transportation revenues can be analyzed by the number of times the fees cover all costs including debt service, by the physical condition of the facility, and by the absence or presence of competing transportation alternatives.

Revenue bonds issued by the New York State Thruway Authority and the New Jersey Turnpike Authority are investment success stories that are counterbalanced by the Chicago Calumet Skyway and the Chesapeake Bay Bridge and Tunnel Authority Series "C" bonds, both of which are in default. The great toll road building activities in the United States seem to be over; most toll road financing now relates to improvements and maintenance of the systems.

In addition to bonds associated with automobile and truck traffic, revenue bonds have financed the construction of many of the airport and port facilities in this country. These bonds should be analyzed in a similar fashion to the toll road facilities: coverage of costs, physical condition, and presence of competition.

COLLEGE AND UNIVERSITY REVENUE BONDS

College and university revenue bonds have a variety of different backings. The security for these bonds can include pledges of various types of income streams of the school: tuition payments, dormitory fees, or parking revenues. If you invest in these bonds, you must know more than the name of the college or university; find out exactly what is pledged for bond service before making any purchase. Maybe you are a graduate of good-old "Mid-State U" and want to buy bonds of this school as a loyal graduate; this may represent fine loyalty to your alma mater, but it can be poor investment strategy. Stay with the large, well-known schools that will be around for years to come. As demographics change, many of the "Mid-State U's" find themselves with declining enrollments and under severe financial pressures. If you want extra security from college and university revenues, look for bonds that are collateralized by the institution's endowment funds. These bonds have marketable securities pledged to pay the principal and interest on the bonds if for any reason the expected source of revenues is insufficient for bond service; collateralized bonds will be discussed in more detail in Chapter 11.

HOUSING REVENUE BONDS

Housing revenue bonds finance a variety of different types of housing needs. Senior citizens housing, low-income housing, and multi-family housing have been constructed with the proceeds of municipal bond sales. The rental payments, often supplemented by various governmental grants, provide the income stream to pay the bonds principal and interest.

Single-family mortgage revenue bonds represent excellent value in housing revenue bonds. These bonds help home buyers finance the purchase of their first home; all the homes are occupied by the owners. A housing authority—typically a state authority—raises money by selling a bond issue. The money is used to purchase mortgages on single-family homes. The portfolio of mortgages that results forms the backing for the bond issue. The mortgages in the portfolio are usually insured by a government agency or a private mortgage insurer. Single-family mortgage revenue bonds provide a basic housing need for the people who are participants in the mortgage programs. These bonds have a built-in equity position because the amount of the outstanding mortgages in the portfolio is assumed to be less than the market value of the homes due to the down payments required by the purchasers. Single-family homes are typically liquid and easily sold to another mortgager if the original purchaser defaults on the mortgage.

If you invest in a single-family mortgage issue sold by the

housing authority of a state, the mortgage portfolio will have an extra element of diversification because the mortgages will be randomly located throughout the state in question. Further strength results from my feeling that a state will support its housing authority in the unlikely event that the authority or a bond issue runs into financial difficulty.

Be careful when investing in any housing revenue bonds selling at substantial premiums, for example, bonds priced in excess of 105. Many housing issues have unusual call provisions that require bonds to be called on any interest payment data from unexpended funds remaining from the initial bond sale or from money received from mortgage prepayments. If interest rates drop, the incentive to refinance existing mortgages increases. This returns money to the housing authority, and this money must be used to call bonds. Many investors have bought a premium bond with what appears to be an attractive yield to the maturity of the bond only to be unpleasantly surprised to have the bond called at par in a few months. The early call of a premium bond at par can greatly reduce the overall yield on the investment. These types of extraordinary calls on housing bonds are often overlooked by both bond dealers and investors.

A subcategory of single-family mortgage revenue bonds with a special call feature provides excellent value for the individual investor. These are the "super sinker" bonds. Few people stay long enough in a home to see the termination of the mortgage. The mortgage burning party has gone the way of the family buggy. Normally people move before the mortgage expires, and the existing mortgage is paid off at the time of the sale of the property. When this happens with a mortgage in a portfolio of a single-family mortgage revenue issue with a super sinker provision, all the proceeds from mortgage prepayments are directed to calling the bonds of one specific maturity. This greatly accelerates the repayment of this particular maturity. For example, the super sinker maturity of a recent issue of the State of Florida Housing Finance Authority was designated as the 2011 maturity. Funds received from the prepayments of mortgages financed by this bond issue will be used to call this one maturity, and the bonds of this maturity should be retired many years before the 2011 maturity. In fact, the average life of these bonds should be approximately four years.

The investment advantage of super sinkers arises from the fact that you receive a yield on the bonds that reflect a maturity of about 10 to 12 years while your money is invested for an average of from four to five years. This allows you to dramatically shorten the period for the return of your invested capital, and at the same time allows you to obtain a yield that reflects a longer term maturity. Super sinkers provide the investor with an increased return (the reward) accompanied by a reduced maturity (the risk).

One word of warning: avoid super sinkers selling at high premiums; the possibilities of very early calls and reduced returns make the premium-priced super sinkers very unattractive investments.

Nearly every state has a housing finance agency that is involved with single-family mortgage revenue bond programs. These bonds are readily available in the secondary market; any of these types of bonds issued by a state housing authority are good investment bets. Super sinkers are periodically available, but the supply of super sinkers will be less than the supply of the more conventional single-family mortgage revenue bonds.

HOSPITAL REVENUE BONDS

Hospital revenue bonds represent one of the most dangerous investment areas for the municipal bond buyer. These bonds are backed by the payments made by patients receiving the services provided by hospitals. As various programs of the federal government have encouraged better and more health care, the construction and enlargement of hospital facilities has greatly increased. The largest part of this expansion has been financed by issuing hospital revenue bonds.

Hospital revenues are risky investments for the following reasons:

1. As an industry, hospitals are labor intensive, high cost providers of services with a generally low margin of coverage for bonds.

2. Most of the income received by hospitals is derived from sources other than the patients themselves, for example, payments from Medicaid and Medicare. These programs can be reduced or changed by the federal or state governments just as the programs were created by these governments. Small reductions in the programs or in the method of reimbursement can create large problems for many hospitals that operate on a very limited income margin over the institution's cost.

3. The stimulation of increased governmental programs plus inexpensive tax-exempt financing via municipal bond sales has led to overbuilding hospital facilities in many areas. Too many beds plus reduced patient stays burden hospitals with high fixed costs and declining revenues. Excessive hospital capacity is basically useless in many instances; patients gravitate to hospitals that are located near their homes for personal convenience. If a hospital closes, it would be difficult to convert the facility into some other type of economic enterprise, unless there is a need in a community for a hotel with small rooms and terrible food.

If you do invest in hospital bonds, I strongly recommend that you look for bonds with credit enhancements. Credit enhancements, which are discussed in Chapter 11, include insurance on the hospital bonds, letters of credit from strong commercial banks, and mortgage insurance from the Federal Housing Administration.

WASTE DISPOSAL REVENUE BONDS

Waste disposal or resource recovery bonds are used to construct facilities to burn garbage. The energy released by the burning process in turn is used to generate electricity. These plants are constructed primarily to provide a method of refuse disposal other than landfill operations; the generation of electricity and sale of recoverable metal scrap are secondary considerations.

The revenue to pay debt service on these bonds comes from the charges levied for the disposal of the garbage plus any funds that are obtained from the sale of electricity or scrap.

These are another class of tax-exempt bonds that are not recommended. I guess you could say that these bonds have a bad odor about them. The record to date for these systems has not been good; several bond issues financing waste disposal projects have gone into default. The technology of the plants is complex, and there is the obvious community opposition to having one of these plants in a neighborhood. If you think this process of garbage disposal will be more viable in the future, invest in the common stock of the plant manufacturers. For the municipal bond investor, these bonds are speculations.

INDUSTRIAL DEVELOPMENT BONDS

Industrial development bonds are tax-exempt corporate bonds. The bonds are issued by a state or municipal authority to build a facility that will be leased to a private corporation. The lease payments made by the private corporation constitute the only backing for the bonds. Industrial development bonds, industrial revenue bonds, and pollution control bonds may have slight legal differences but for the investor, they are all the same: these bonds are credits of a corporation and are only as strong as the corporation making the lease payments. Analyze these bonds solely on the strength of the corporation backing the bond.

Be especially careful to avoid nonrated industrial development bonds. Many highly speculative, relative small issues of these types of bonds have been sold by unscrupulous bond dealers using the following sales approach. You are offered the bonds of a state's economic development authority; the sales representative emphasizes the name of the state agency giving the impression of a guarantee on the bonds by the state or one of its agencies. You are not properly informed that the issue is for the Widget Manufacturing Project. The bond has absolutely no backing from the state and is only as good a credit as is the Widget Manufacturing Company. Here—as with all revenue bonds—you must know exactly what is the source of the funds that will pay the interest and principal.

HIGHLIGHTS REGARDING REVENUE BONDS

1. Know exactly what activity is providing the income to repay the bonds. Do not be satisfied with knowing only the name of the state or municipal authority issuing the bond.

2. Term bonds and dollar bonds are an excellent way to accumulate round lots of municipal bonds.

3. Invest in utility bonds of existing systems. Avoid systems with a heavy dependence on nuclear power.

4. Water and sewer revenue bonds of economically strong communities represent excellent value.

5. Super sinkers give you the ability to invest your funds for a shorter time but obtain yields that reflect a longer period.

6. "Think big" when investing in university bonds. Only purchase securities issued by large well-known schools.

7. Hospital bonds and waste disposal bonds should be avoided by most municipal investors.

8. Industrial development bonds are tax-exempt corporate debt. You are betting solely on the corporation when you invest in these bonds. Never purchase a nonrated industrial development bond.

7

lessening
the tax bite

Despite the alleged simplification of the tax codes by the passage of the Tax Reform Bill of 1986, taxes still remain a complicated subject. Tax regulations continue to support an entire industry of accountants, lawyers, preparers, and consultants who work solely on tax-related matters. Regardless of this complexity, municipal bonds still are the easiest and surest way for the individual investor to lessen the tax bite. The interest you receive from municipal bonds is free from federal income taxes; however, some taxpayers may find themselves with a tax liability for some municipal bond interest that is subject to alternative minimum taxes. With a little planning, you can also avoid paying most state and local taxes on municipal bond interest.

HOW MUCH TAX DO YOU PAY?

Your total tax bite is much larger than you would suspect. If you were to add the income taxes paid to the federal government; the income, sales, and property taxes paid to state and local governments; and the taxes paid whenever you purchase gasoline, cigarettes, or liquor to the myriad of hidden indirect taxes you pay, you would come to the conclusion that taxes take a very heavy share indeed of your disposable income—despite the "tax relief" provided by the recent tax legislation. The more you appreciate how large the tax burden, the more the incentive you will have in reducing the bite.

If you are investing in municipal bonds, you should analyze the marginal tax rate you pay on taxable income. The marginal tax rate is the highest rate you pay on any one dollar of taxable income. Your marginal tax rate is the rate you pay on the last dollar you earn during the tax year; if you can shift this last dollar of income from one that is taxable to one that is tax exempt, you will be maximizing your spendable income. Of course, all the dollars you earn are not subject to the same tax rate. Deductions allow a certain base of income to escape taxes altogether.

As your taxable income grows, the tax rates also increase. Figure 7.1 shows the tax brackets for federal income taxes under the 1986 Tax Reform Bill. Starting in 1988, most investors in municipal bonds will find themselves in the 28% or 33% brackets. Every $1.00 you earn from municipal bonds is more valuable to you because is saves you 28¢ or 33¢ of taxes that you would have paid to the federal government if the income had been derived from a taxable investment. This reduction in federal taxes is only the first saving in taxes as we shall see later in this chapter when we discuss state and local taxes.

TAX EQUIVALENTS

In most market conditions, the rate of interest you receive from municipal bonds is less than the rate of interest you receive from taxable fixed return investments of similar quality and maturity. This is logical as the interest from municipals is free from federal income taxes, whereas the interest from securities like U.S. Treasury bonds, corporate bonds, and bank certificates is subject to federal income taxes.

There are occasions when market conditions allow you to invest in municipal bonds yielding a *higher* return than taxable bonds. During mid-year 1986, good quality long-term tax-exempt municipal bonds were yielding more than long-term taxable U.S. Treasury bonds. This type of market condition represents a bonanza for investors in municipal bonds.

It is easy to determine the trade-off or the equivalent between a tax-exempt rate of interest and a taxable one. If you divide the tax-exempt rate by the reciprocal of your marginal tax rate, you will have the taxable equivalent. For example, assume you are in the 28% tax bracket and are considering investing in a municipal bond selling at par and paying a 7% return. The taxable equivalent would be:

$$7.00\% \div [1.00 - .28] = 7.00/.72 = 9.72\%.$$

FIGURE 7.1. Federal Individual Income Tax Rates for Taxable Income

	Joint Return		Single Return		Head of Household	
For 1987	$0–3,000	11%	$0–1,800	11%	$0–2,550	11%
	3,001–28,000	15%	1,801–16,800	15%	2,551–23,800	15%
	28,001–45,000	28%	16,801–27,000	28%	23,801–38,250	28%
	45,001–90,000	35%	27,001–54,000	35%	38,251–76,500	35%
	Over 90,000	38.5%	Over 54,000	38.5%	Over 76,500	38.5%
For 1988	$0–29,750	15%	$0–17,850	15%	$0–25,290	15%
	29,751–71,900	28%	17,851–43,150	28%	25,291–61,115	28%
	71,901–171,090	33%	43,151–100,480	33%	61,116–148,709	33%
	Over 171,090	28%	Over 100,480	28%	Over 148,709	28%

Source: Laventhol and Horwath, "Legislative Alert," Aug. 25, 1986.

This means that a 7% municipal bond and a 9.72% taxable bond provide the same return after federal income taxes if you are in the 28% tax bracket. If taxable investments are paying *less than* 9.72%, you will receive a higher return on the 7% municipal bond.

If you want to know the tax exempt equivalent of a taxable investment, multiply the taxable rate by the reciprocal of your marginal tax rate. For example, the tax exempt equivalent of an 8% taxable bond, assuming your maximum tax rate is 28%, would be:

$$8.00\% \times (1.00 - .28) = 8.00\% \times .72 = 5.76\%$$

In this case, if your option is to receive 8.00% taxable and more than 5.76% from a comparable municipal security, invest in the municipal. In the vast majority of market conditions, investors in the middle and higher tax brackets will find a decidedly greater after tax return from municipal bonds than from taxable fixed income investments.

Figure 7.2 shows Tax Equivalent Tables which will allow you to quickly find the equivalent between tax-exempt and taxable bonds. For example, if you are in the 33% tax bracket, the table shows that an 8% tax-exempt bond is the same as an 11.9% taxable bond. If you cannot obtain at least an 11.9% return from a taxable bond, invest in the tax-exempt bond at 8%.

ALTERNATIVE MINIMUM TAXES

The Tax Reform Bill of 1986 makes provisions for the first time for direct federal taxation of some municipal bond interest. Starting in 1987, interest from "nonessential" municipal bonds issued after August 7, 1986 may be subject to an alternative minimum tax.

A nonessential bond is one where more than 10% of the bond

FIGURE 7.2. Tax Equivalent Tables

Tax Bracket	15%	28%	33%	35%	38.5%
Tax Exempt Rate			*Taxable Equivalents*		
3.0	3.5	4.2	4.5	4.6	4.9
3.5	4.1	4.9	5.2	5.4	5.7
4.0	4.7	5.6	6.0	6.2	6.5
4.5	5.3	6.3	6.7	6.9	7.3
5.0	5.9	6.9	7.5	7.7	8.1
5.5	6.5	7.6	8.2	8.5	8.9
6.0	7.1	8.3	9.0	9.2	9.8
6.5	7.6	9.0	9.7	10.0	10.6
7.0	8.2	9.7	10.4	10.8	11.4
7.5	8.8	10.4	11.2	11.5	12.2
8.0	9.4	11.1	11.9	12.3	13.0
8.5	10.0	11.8	12.7	13.1	13.8
9.0	10.6	12.5	13.4	13.8	14.6
9.5	11.2	13.2	14.2	14.6	15.4
10.0	11.8	13.9	14.9	15.4	16.3
11.0	12.9	15.3	16.4	16.9	17.9
12.0	14.1	16.7	17.9	18.5	19.5

proceeds is used for other than a public purpose. Examples of nonessential bonds include single family mortgage revenue bonds, multifamily housing bonds, industrial development bonds, and student loan bonds. You have to include the interest you receive from these nonessential bonds in determining whether or not you are subject to an alternative minimum tax. If you are subject to an alternative minimum tax, you will pay a 21% tax on the interest you receive from nonessential municipal bonds.

This provision applies *only* to nonessential bonds issued after August 7, 1986. Nonessential bonds in your portfolio that were purchased before that date escape this possible tax liability. Nonessential bonds you may have purchased after August 7, 1986 also escape the tax provision if the bonds in question were issued before August 7, 1986.

This feature of the tax regulations should not be a problem for the vast majority of individual investors since it is easy to avoid this tax bite. If you are subject to alternative minimum taxes, simply avoid purchasing nonessential bonds issued after August 7, 1986; your bond dealer can advise you as to whether or not a particular bond is "essential" or "nonessential." If you are not subject to alternative minimum taxes, you can reap the benefit of this tax provision. Nonessential bonds will tend to yield greater returns than essential bonds due to the possible tax liability associated with the nonessential bonds. As a result, the investor who is not subject to an alternative minimum tax can obtain a higher return from a nonessential bond than would have been the case without the potential tax liability.

STATE AND LOCAL INCOME TAXES

Some fortunate investors live in states that do not have state or local income taxes. However, the vast majority of us find ourselves subject to demands from state and local tax collectors. Municipal bonds help reduce the tax bite claimed by state and local taxing units. "Local" governments include cities and counties that levy income taxes; because these jurisdictions usually follow their respective state tax regulations regarding municipal bonds, I will refer to only "state" income taxes in the remainder of this chapter.

The general rule applied to state taxation of municipal bond interest is that the interest you receive on a municipal bond issued by a given state or any of its political subdivisions is free from the taxes of that state. However, the states usually tax the interest you receive on an out-of-state bond; this is the case in 35 of the 50 states. Three states tax the interest received on *all* municipal bonds both out-of-state bonds and bonds issued within the state itself. Five states and the District of Columbia totally exclude all municipal bond interest from their income taxes. The

FIGURE 7.3. State Taxation of Municipal Bond Interest

Exempt In-State Bonds; Tax Out-of-State Bonds

Alabama	Arizona	Arkansas
California	Colorado	Connecticut
Delaware	Georgia	Hawaii
Idaho	Kansas	Kentucky
Louisiana	Maine	Maryland
Massachusetts	Michigan	Minnesota
Mississippi	Missouri	Montana
New Hampshire	New Jersey	New York
North Carolina	North Dakota	Ohio
Oklahoma	Oregon	Pennsylvania
Rhode Island	South Carolina	Tennessee
	Virginia	West Virginia

Tax Both In-State and Out-of-State Bonds

Illinois	Iowa	Wisconsin

Exempt Both In-State and Out-of-State Bonds

District of Columbia	Indiana	Nebraska
New Mexico	Utah	Vermont

States Without State Income Taxes

Alaska	Florida	Nevada
South Dakota	Texas	Washington
	Wyoming	

lucky residents of seven states pay no state income tax. Figure 7.3 shows the category for each state regarding taxation of municipal bond income.

For the 35 states that exempt their own bonds from taxation but tax the bonds of their sister states, if you know the state income tax rate, you can determine the value of state income tax exemption on a municipal bond. Column 2 of Figure 7.4 shows the maximum income tax rate levied by the 35 states in question. In general, a resident of one of these states reaches the maximum state income tax burden fairly quickly so that the maximum rate is a good gauge of measuring state tax burden for most investors in municipal bonds.

FIGURE 7.4. State Income Tax Rates and Yield Advantages

State	Maximum Income Tax Rate	Yield Advantage in 28% Bracket	Yield Advantage in 33% Bracket
Alabama	5%	27	25
Arizona	8%	43	40
Arkansas	7%	38	35
California	11%	59	55
Colorado	8%	43	40
Connecticut	13%	70	65
Delaware	13.5%	73	68
Georgia	6%	32	30
Hawaii	11%	59	55
Idaho	7.5%	41	38
Kansas	9%	49	45
Kentucky	6%	32	30
Louisiana	6%	32	30
Maine	10%	54	50
Maryland	5%	27	25
Massachusetts	10%	54	50
Michigan	4.6%	25	23
Minnesota	16%	86	80
Mississippi	5%	27	25
Missouri	6%	32	30
Montana	11%	59	55
New Hampshire	5%	27	25
New Jersey	3.5%	19	18
New York	13.5%	73	68
NYS & NYC Combined	17.8%	96	89
North Carolina	7%	38	35
North Dakota	9%	49	45
Ohio	9.5%	51	48
Oklahoma	6%	32	30
Oregon	10%	54	50
Pennsylvania	2.2%	12	11
Rhode Island	8%	43	40
South Carolina	7%	38	35
Tennessee	6%	32	30
Virginia	5.75%	31	29
West Virginia	13%	70	65

Sources: State Tax Handbook, Commerce Clearing House, Inc., Chicago, Il.; Guide to State and Local Taxation of Municipal Bonds, Gabriele, Hueglin & Cashman, Inc., New York, NY.

If you know your state income tax rate, you can determine what the yield advantage of an in-state bond would be over an out-of-state bond. For example, if you are a Massachusetts resident considering investing in a 7.5% municipal bond issued by a Massachusetts municipality, what would be the return needed from a bond of similar quality and maturity issued by a New Hampshire municipality to equalize the 7.5% return from the Massachusetts bond? Because, as a Massachusetts resident, you have to pay a tax to Massachusetts on the income you receive from the New Hampshire bond, you would need a higher return from the New Hampshire bond to compensate for the Massachusetts tax. The problem becomes more complicated because the Massachusetts tax that is paid on the New Hampshire bond interest becomes a deduction for federal income tax purposes thereby reducing the effective cost of the Massachusetts tax. The key to this question is "yield advantage." Yield advantage is the number of basis points you must receive from an out-of-state bond to pay in-state income tax liability on the interest you receive from the out-of-state bond. The following formula shows how to find the approximate yield advantage:

$$C \times STR \times [1.00 - FTR] = YA$$

where

C = interest rate of the out-of-state bond

STR = in-state tax rate

FTR = federal income tax rate

YA = yield advantage

For example, assume you are a Massachusetts resident in both the 10% Massachusetts income tax bracket and the 28% federal income tax bracket. You are considering investing in a 7.5% bond issued by New Hampshire. The yield advantage would be:

$$7.5 \times .10 \times [1.00 - .28] = .54, \text{ or 54 basis points}$$

This means that your return from the New Hampshire bond will be 6.96% [7.50 − .54] after paying Massachusetts taxes on the New Hampshire bond. In this case you would need 54 basis points additional yield from the out-of-state bond to equate the yield from an in-state bond. The last two columns of Figure 7.4 show the yield advantage in basis points for the various state income taxes for both the 28% and 33% federal income tax brackets. These yield advantages are based on a 7.5% interest rate; for a different interest rate, simply use the formula shown in the preceding paragraph to determine the yield advantage for your state and the bond in question.

The yield advantages shown in Figure 7.4 reflect only income tax rates of the various states. State personal property taxes, intangible taxes, and unearned income taxes are not included. Investors should consult their tax advisors concerning their particular state tax considerations.

Before investing in a municipal bond you should know the yield advantage. Many times you can obtain a *higher* return from an out-of-state bond even after paying an in-state tax; this is especially so if you live in a state with a relatively low state income tax rate.

When discussing state taxes, you should be aware of a special group of bonds that are free of federal income taxes plus income taxes levied by any state. These are the bonds issued by United States commonwealths and possessions. Bonds issued by Puerto Rico, the U.S. Virgin Islands, and Guam are free of all state income taxes, even those levied by states that tax out-of-state municipal bonds and those levied by states that tax their own state's municipal bonds.

OTHER CATEGORIES OF FEDERAL TAXES

Municipal bonds are treated as any other type of investment when considering taxes other than income taxes. There is no tax advantage to owning a municipal bond when considering federal capital gains taxes, estate taxes, or gift taxes.

If you purchase a municipal bond at a discount and redeem it at maturity for its face value, the appreciation is taxable capital gains. There are two exceptions to this rule. First, "zero coupon" municipal bonds—which pay no interest—are issued at a substantial discount from their face value; the appreciation of a zero coupon municipal bond is considered tax-exempt income. Second, some municipal bonds are issued at a discount with a lower rate of interest than the going market rate. These bonds are called "original issue discount" bonds (OIDs), and like zero coupon bonds, their appreciation to par is tax exempt. If you invest in this latter type of bond, make sure that the bond confirmation you receive from your broker identifies the bond as an original issue discount bond.

Remember that the appreciation of most municipal bonds you purchase at a discount is subject to tax, but the amortization of the premium of a municipal bond is never a tax deduction.

MUNICIPALS AND SOCIAL SECURITY BENEFITS

If you are receiving social security benefits and if your income from all sources exceeds certain base amounts, your social security benefits may be subject to federal income taxes. Unfortunately for many senior citizens, municipal bond interest is included in the base to determine total income. This can result in retired people finding their social security benefits taxed and their total tax bill increased because they receive interest from municipal bonds or from tax-exempt bond funds. If your income from all sources, including municipal bond interest, exceeds $25,000 for a single taxpayer or $32,000 for joint filers, part of your social security benefits will probably be subject to taxation.

Here's an example showing how social security benefits may be taxable. Mr. and Mrs. Jones receive $6000 a year from social security. In addition, they receive pension benefits and other taxable income totalling $30,000. The Jones' have invested in several unit investment trusts and own some municipal bonds; their tax-exempt investments produce $8500 of interest a year. Mr. and Mrs. Jones find that half of their $6000 social security benefits is subject to taxation because their income from all sources—$38,500—exceeds the $32,000 base for taxpayers filing joint returns.

You may believe that this does not represent a tax on municipal bond income. However, I think that if the receipt of income from one source (municipal bond income) increases your tax bill from some other source of income (social security benefits in this case), you are subject to an indirect tax on your tax-exempt income. Furthermore, because the Jones' have to report some of their social security benefits as taxable income, they also are required to list *all* municipal bond interest they received on their Form 1040 when they file their tax returns. These increased taxes and reporting requirements are another classic example of the "camel getting the nose in the tent." We all know what the camel wants after getting his nose in the tent.

Several law suits have been filed against the federal government challenging the increased taxation of social security benefits based on the receipt of municipal bond interest. Whether or not this indirect taxation of municipal securities will continue in the future is for the courts to decide. In the meantime, while the courts decide, Washington collects.

BROKER INFORMATIONAL REPORTING

One tax-related topic that all investors should be aware of concerns reporting requirements involving municipal bond transactions. Under the terms of the Tax Equity and Fiscal Responsibility Act of 1982, any time you sell a municipal bond or note, the sale proceeds are reported to the federal government by the bank or broker that handled the transaction. This reporting also includes the proceeds from a maturing tax-exempt bond or note, for the redemption at maturity is considered to be a sale of the security back to the issuing municipality.

You will receive a copy of a Form 1099 with the details of the sale transaction from your bank or broker, and the same information will be forwarded to the Internal Revenue Service. Individuals must reconcile these Form 1099s on Schedule D of their tax returns.

Broker informational reporting, as the requirement is officially called, is designed to catch municipal securities that have passed from one owner to another without the payment of gift or estate taxes, and to improve compliance with reporting capital gains on municipal securities sold at a profit or on municipal securities purchased at a discount and redeemed at par at maturity.

MUNICIPAL BONDS, BORROWED FUNDS, AND TAXES

If an individual borrows money and uses it to purchase municipal bonds, the interest on the borrowed funds is not a tax-deductible expense. If this were not the case, individuals in a high tax bracket would be able to make arbitrage profits by borrowing money and investing in municipals. For example, if you are in the 28% tax bracket and borrow money at 10%, the after tax cost of the borrowed money is 7.2% if the cost of the borrowing is tax deductible. If you use the money that costs you 7.2% after tax to obtain an 8% tax-free return, you are making a gain on the transaction even though the 10% initial cost of the loan is greater than the 8% return on the municipal bond.

Individuals can borrow money and still invest in municipal bonds. You can have borrowings related to your residence, to personal expenditures, and to business assets and activities and hold municipal bonds.

Between the two extremes of disallowing costs of borrowing and allowing them, there is a gray area. In this gray area, the IRS will try to establish a connection between certain types of borrowings and investing in municipal securities to the detriment of the investor. For example, suppose you currently own municipal bonds, and you borrow money to buy common stock. In this case, you run the risk of the IRS connecting the money you borrowed to buy the common stock to carrying the municipal bonds. You may argue that there is no time relationship between the existing municipal bonds and the new borrowing for the purchase of common stock. The IRS will argue that you could have sold the municipals and used the proceeds to buy the common stock. If you think this reasoning is a little twisted, remember that the IRS has never demonstrated affection for tax-exempt securities. The IRS will try to find a connection and use this indirect connection to disallow the deductibility of the cost of borrowed funds.

Another gray area arises from the use of municipals as collateral for a loan. The IRS tends to make no distinction between borrowing to invest in tax-exempt bonds and borrowing against municipal bonds in your portfolio. Here again, the logic of the IRS is that you could have sold your municipal bonds and avoided the borrowing.[1]

TAX POINTS TO REMEMBER

1. Municipal bonds are still a simple, effective way for individual investors to reduce their tax bite. The new Tax Reform Bill has placed many restrictions on tax shelters, so many in fact, that municipal bonds have become the best game in town for investors trying to avoid the tax collectors.

2. Before making an investment, know the taxable equivalent of the municipal security you are considering purchasing and compare the taxable equivalent with alternative taxable investments.

3. Determine the yield advantage of out-of-state bonds to obtain the best return from either an in-state or an out-of-state bond.

4. Be aware of situations in which the IRS could disallow borrowing costs that are related to buying or carrying municipal bonds.

5. Taxes are a complicated and ever changing situation. Although the information in this chapter is taken from reliable sources, I urge you to consult your tax advisor as to questions about taxes and your tax liabilities.

8

unraveling
the mystery of
bond math

The mathematics of bonds pose a puzzle for many individual investors. A great number of the technical questions about bonds that I receive from investors involve some aspect of bond mathematics. The math puzzle is like many other types of puzzles: it is composed of a number of small pieces. If you examine each piece separately, the puzzle soon becomes clear.

There are four major parts to the mathematic puzzle for municipal bonds:

1. Pricing
2. Interest
3. Yields
4. Call features

In turn, each of these four major parts is divided into several subcategories.

PRICING

Let's assume that you want to buy $10,000 worth of bonds. The $10,000 is the principal or par or face value of the bond; it is the amount of money you will receive when the bonds are redeemed at their maturity. In the bond market, this transaction is referred to as a purchase of "10 bonds," as a bond is assumed to have $1000 par value.

If the bonds are priced at 100, the bonds are priced at par. Par and 100 are identical. If you buy 10 bonds and you pay par, you pay $10,000 for the face value of the bonds. At maturity you will receive $10,000 for your bonds.

Many times, bonds are offered to investors at prices other than par. Just as stock prices change, bond prices change to reflect different market conditions. The main reason why bond prices change is interest rate fluctuations. If interest rates go down, the price of municipal bonds goes up; if interest rates go up, the price of bonds goes down.

If a bond is priced above par, the bond is selling at a premium. The premium price of a bond is a reflection of the higher interest rate, or coupon, that the bond is paying. Using our example of buying 10 bonds, if you pay 102 for the bonds, the bonds are selling at a premium. The price for the $10,000 par value of bonds will be $10,200, that is, $10,000 times 102%. At maturity, the bonds will be redeemed for $10,000. The $200 premium will not be returned to the investor; the premium will be recouped in the higher interest payments that you receive each year you hold the bond. The amortization of the premium results in a return on your investment that is numerically lower than the interest rate on the bonds. Unfortunately, this $200 reduction is not a capital loss for tax purposes.

If you buy your bonds for a price below par, the bonds are selling at a discount. Following our example, an investor buying 10 bonds at a price of 90 would pay $9000, that is, $10,000 multiplied by 90%. The increase from $9000 to $10,000 at maturity results in a higher return on your investment than the interest rate on the bonds. If you hold the bonds until they mature, the $1000 appreciation in price at maturity is subject to capital gains taxes. There is no tax advantage from buying premium bonds, but there is a tax liability from buying discount bonds.

Why do bonds sell at premiums or discounts? Assume the current market rate for a 20-year bond is 8%. You purchase this bond at par or 100. The 8% interest rate on your bond is fixed for the next 20 years; it will not fluctuate. Time passes and market conditions change; newly issued 20-year bonds return 7%. Because your bond is still paying 8%, it is worth more than the newly issued bonds paying 7%. There is some price—and this price will be over 100—at which your bond paying 8% will equate to the 7% return on the new bond. In a similar fashion, if interest rates were to increase to 9%, your 8% bond would be worth less than par in order to recognize that its return is less than the new higher interest rate in the market. The vast majority of price fluctuations in tax-exempt bonds reflect changing interest rates and have absolutely nothing to do with changes in the inherent quality of the municipal bond itself.

ACCRUED INTEREST

A bond is very much like a windup clock. The clock is wound up; it starts to tick and will keep ticking for some period and then stop. A bond acts in the same fashion. It starts to "tick," that is, to pay interest; it pays interest for a period, and at maturity, the bond stops paying interest. For as long as the bond is ticking, it is accumulating interest, or in the language of the bond market, the bond is accruing interest.

Interest starts accruing on the dated date of the bond. This is the date the bond becomes alive and starts to tick. In six months, the bond will pay interest for the first six months of its life. Each six months thereafter, the bond will pay interest until the bond matures. At maturity, when our bond stops ticking, the last interest payment will be paid and the bond will be redeemed.

Because the bond pays interest only on six-month intervals, what happens if a bond is bought or sold between interest dates? The buyer of the bond pays the seller of the bond the amount of interest that has accumulated, or accrued, on the bond since its last interest payment. This accrued interest is added to the price of the bond transaction and will raise the total purchase price of the bond. You can expect to pay accrued interest whether you buy a bond at par, at a discount, or at a premium. The new holder of the bond, the buyer, will receive six months worth of interest at the next interest payment date even though the buyer has not held the bond for the full six-month period. This extra interest will return the accrued interest that the buyer paid the seller at the time of the transaction.

Let's look at an example of how accrued interest works. You

buy $10,000 principal value of bonds; the bonds have an 8% coupon and will pay $800 a year. Because bonds pay interest semi-annually, the interest payments will be $400 each six months. If the bonds you are buying have interest payment dates of January 1 and July 1, on these two dates $400 of interest is due to you the bondholder. The entire $400 will be paid on these dates to the current bondholder, if that bondholder held the bond for the full six months or only a portion of the six-month period (Figure 8.1). Each January and July, $400 is paid by the issuer to the bondholder. What happens if you buy these bonds for settlement on April 1, 1987, midway between the interest payment dates? On April 1, $200 will be paid by the buyer to the seller as part of the purchase transaction, because the interest that has accrued on the bonds for January, February, and March belongs to the seller. On July 1, 1987, the buyer receives $400 from the issuer. The buyer has owned the bond for only three months yet receives six months interest. The $400 received on July 1, 1987 by the buyer represents the return of the $200 accrued interest paid to the seller of April 1, 1987, plus the interest that accrued on the bonds for April, May, and June. If you pay accrued interest as part of a bond purchase, you will have all the accrued interest

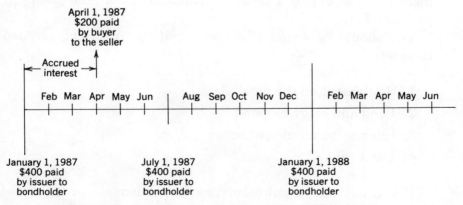

Figure 8.1 Bond interest payments: $10,000, 8% bonds.

returned to you at the time of the next scheduled interest payment.

Accrued interest is separate and distinct from the "price" of the bond which can be par, a premium, or a discount. Following with our example, if you buy $10,000 principal value of bonds at par for settlement of April 1, the total payment will be:

Principal $10,000 @ 100	$10,000.00
Accrued interest	200.00
Total payment	$10,200.00

If you buy your bonds at a premium price of 102 for April 1 settlement, the payment will be:

Principal $10,000 @ 102	$10,200.00
Accrued interest	200.00
Total payment	$10,400.00

Notice that the accrued interest is the same in both cases. If the bonds were purchased at a discount, the accrued interest would also be $200. Accrued interest is a function of the interest rate on the bond and the time period since that last interest payment was made. It is a separate transaction from the price you pay for a bond.

You should be aware of a few variations involving accrued interest:

1. Settlement on the dated date
2. Long and short coupons
3. Interest on municipal notes
4. Day count

If you buy municipal securities for settlement on the dated date, there will be no accrued interest because you are purchasing the securities on the day the interest starts to accrue. This sometimes happens when you buy a newly issued bond; it is a more common occurrence with newly issued tax-exempt notes.

Even though bonds pay interest every six months, the first interest payment that is made on a bond after it is issued may be other than six months. If it is more than six months, the first coupon is called a "long coupon," and the amount of accrued interest will be more than six months. Long coupons are normally between six months and one year in duration. "Short coupons" result from the first interest payment being less than six months. Only the first interest payment will be long or short. After the initial payment of a long or short coupon, interest will be paid every six months. An investor only has to be aware that these odd interest payments can exist with bonds that have been issued within the past year. Ask your bond dealer if the bond you are purchasing has a long or short first coupon.

Municipal notes, which will be discussed in Chapter 10, are short-term borrowings of states and municipalities. The maturity of notes is usually one year or less. As these securities are short-term in nature, all the interest is paid at maturity. Even if the note has a maturity of one year, there will be no interest payment until it matures. Notes can accumulate a considerable amount of accrued interest if you purchase the notes close to their maturity date.

You should be aware of one final facet about municipal bond interest. These securities have their interest figured on the base of each month having 30 days; therefore, a year for a municipal bond has 360 days. You lend your money to the state or municipality for 365 days a year and get paid only 360 days interest. On a 25-year bond, that's the loss of about four months interest. This 360-day year is an anachronistic holdover from the days when accrued interest was calculated by hand; there is no justification for this practice existing today when we have electronic calculators and computers to perform bond computations. However, if you are trying to verify the accrued interest on a municipal bond transaction, remember that the days used to determine the accrued interest are counted on a 30-day month.

YIELDS

Municipal bonds are an unusual product in that most municipal bonds are not priced in terms of dollars and cents when they are bought or sold. With municipal bonds, the cryptic concept of yield replaces dollars and cents. Yields tell you the overall return that you receive on a municipal bond investment. Yields take into account the interest payments you receive; the time the bond has to run to maturity; and the price—par, premium, or discount—you pay for the bond. Yield is the concept that adjusts all outstanding bonds to current market conditions. Yield allows bonds with large coupons selling at premiums to trade in the marketplace with bonds of small coupons selling at discounts. Yield permits the marketplace to distinguish between similar bonds with different maturities. Yield is the "lingua franca" of the municipal bond market.

Yield, basis, and return are three terms that tend to be used interchangeably in the municipal market. These three terms mean basically the same thing when you are investing in tax-exempt securities.

A bond has two fixed components: interest rate and maturity. Given these two fixed components, if a bond is priced to yield the investor a particular return, the dollar price of the bond can be determined. If a tax-exempt bond is offered in dollar terms, the yield can be determined. Because interest rate and maturity are fixed, yield determines the dollar price, and the dollar price determines the yield.

You should be aware of three different yields:

1. Current yield
2. Yield to maturity
3. Yield to average life

Current yield is a simple concept. If you buy a bond at some dollar price, X, and it pays annual interest of Y, current yield is Y divided by X. For example, you pay 112 for a bond with a 10% coupon; the current yield is 10 divided by 112, or 8.93%. If you buy a 4% bond at a discount price of 75, the current yield is 4 divided by 75, or 5.33%. Current yield takes neither the maturity date of the bond nor the premium or discount you might pay into account. For this reason, current yield is a poor way to measure the return on a municipal bond. A bond selling at a premium pays what appears to be an attractive current yield, as the current yield disregards the decline in value of the bond as it approaches maturity. Be careful that a less than scrupulous bond dealer does not try to sell you a bond based on its apparent high current yield. The high yield you receive today is counterbalanced by the high premium you pay and the decline in value due to the amortization of the premium.

The better concept of yield for the municipal bond investor is yield to maturity. Yield to maturity takes into account the price you pay for the bond, the interest rate on the bond, and the time to its maturity. Yield to maturity acknowledges the decline associated with the amortization of the premium on a bond and the gain associated with the accretion of a discount bond. Unfortunately, because the yield to maturity takes all these factors into account, problems involving yield to maturity are mathematically complicated. The formulas used to determine yield to maturity are too complex for the average individual investor buying municipal bonds. Appendix B shows samples of the major formulas involving municipal bonds. It is more important for you to understand the concept of yield to maturity than to know how to use these formulas. Yield to maturity must be shown on the confirmation that the bond dealer provides you after each transaction. Make sure you know the yield to maturity before you make a purchase or sale of municipal bonds.

If you would like to be able to figure yield to maturity yourself, there are two methods available. Small calculators can be purchased that are programmed to figure yield to maturity. In addition, basis books containing bond yield tables are obtainable in libraries and from larger bookstores. Appendix C shows a sample of bond yield tables and how to use them.

Municipal bond investors will find the following examples a good method of determining the approximate yield to maturity for discount or premium bonds.

Example 1: Premium Bonds

Maturity value of bond	$1000
Price @ 102	1020
Premium	20
Time to maturity	9 years
Interest rate	8%

To figure the approximate yield to maturity use the formula:

$$\frac{\text{Maturity value} \times \text{interest rate} - \dfrac{\text{premium}}{\text{years to maturity}}}{\text{Purchase price}}$$

Using the figures from Example 1, we obtain:

$$\frac{1000 \times .08 - \left(\dfrac{20}{9}\right)}{1020} = \frac{77.78}{1020} = .0763, \text{ or } 7.63\%$$

The result of this equation is an approximation; the yield to maturity by using a bond calculator would be 7.69%.

Example 2: Discount Bonds

Maturity value of bond	$1000
Price @ 98½	985
Discount	15

Time to maturity 5 years

Interest rate 4¾%

With discount bonds, the formula changes to:

$$\frac{\text{Maturity value} \times \text{interest rate} + \dfrac{\text{discount}}{\text{years to maturity}}}{\text{Purchase price}}$$

Using the above example, the results are:

$$\frac{1000 \times .0475 + \left(\dfrac{15}{5}\right)}{985} = \frac{50.5}{985} = .0512, \text{ or } 5.12\%$$

By using a bond calculator, the more accurate answer of 5.19% would be obtained.

These formulas are good approximations for discounts or premiums up to about three points, or $30, per bond. The formulas become less accurate as the amount of the premium or discount increases.

As we saw in Chapter 6, many term bonds have sinking funds which result in some bonds being redeemed each year before the indicated final maturity of the bond. This shortens the average life of the bond issue and changes the yield you can receive on bonds that have a sinking fund feature.

Let me show you a simplified example of how a sinking fund operates. Assume a $100 million municipal issue is sold with all the bonds having a maturity of 20 years. After 10 years, the sinking fund starts to operate, and $10 million worth of bonds must be redeemed by the issuer each year from the 11th to the 20th year. Obviously, this bond issue does not have a 20-year average maturity; only a small percentage of these bonds will be redeemed at their final 20-year maturity. Based on the mathematics of the bonds being called for the sinking fund, the average life of the entire issue will not be 20 years, but approximately 15½ years. There is no guarantee that the particular bonds you buy will have a maturity of 15½ years, but based upon probability, that is the expected average life of the bond issue. If you invest in bonds with sinking funds, you should know the average life of the remaining bonds in the issue and the yield to this average life in addition to knowing the yield to maturity. For example, assume you buy a 6% bond at a price of 75; the final maturity of this bond is 20 years but the sinking fund will reduce the average life to 15½ years. In this transaction the yield to maturity is 8.65%, but very few bonds will go to this final maturity. The yield to the average life is 9.03%, which represents a substantial improvement. In considering yields on bonds with sinking funds, using the yield to the average life is a better method of analyzing your return and of making an investment decision than would be using yield to maturity.

This concept becomes especially interesting when looking at super sinker municipal bonds. These bonds were described in Chapter 6. Super sinkers have an expected life that is considerably shorter than their stated maturity. The expected life of these bonds is in the four- to five-year range even though their stated maturity may be in the 20- to 30-year range. When figuring the yields on super sinker bonds, it is much more logical to use their average expected life than their final maturity.

CALLABLE BONDS

The last topic to be examined when discussing bond mathematics involves bonds with call features. Most municipal bonds that are issued with maturities in excess of 10 years will have call features. The call feature allows the state or municipality that sold the bonds the option to redeem the bonds before their stated maturity. Whether or not your callable bonds will be called is not your decision but rather that of the issuer. You should be aware of any call features that exist on municipal bonds before you make an investment.

Bonds may be called at par or at slight premiums. For example, a newly issued bond may be callable in 10 years at a price of 103 or in 15 years at 100. The vast majority of municipal bonds that have call features require the issuer to redeem the bonds at least at par; however, there are some issues that can be called below par, for example, original issue discount bonds and zero coupon bonds. For this discussion of callable bonds, I will assume the more common situation of bonds being callable at par or at a premium.

If you purchase a callable bond selling at par or at a discount, the mathematics present no complication. Yields are figured the same way as if the bonds were noncallable, and the yield would reflect the bond's final maturity. If a discount bond is called, you reap a little windfall. You had purchased the bond based upon the assumption that it would go to maturity; now the call of the bond returns your principal quicker thereby increasing the overall yield.

The complications of callable bonds arise when you buy a callable bond selling at a premium. In this case, you must be aware that if the bond is called, your yield could be reduced below the yield you had expected to receive if you had held the bond to maturity. A callable bond selling at a premium must be priced in such a way as to insure the investor that the yield that is expected to maturity will be realized even if the bond should be called before maturity. In figuring the yields on callable bonds, the yield must be figured to both maturity and the call date. If the yield to the call date results in a lower dollar price than would result from the yield to maturity, the purchaser of the bond is entitled to the lower of the two dollar prices. This lower dollar price protects the purchaser against the yield being diminished due to a call taking place. If the bond is not called and goes to its final maturity, the lower price results in increased yield.

For example, suppose you purchase a 9% municipal bond maturing in 20 years to yield 8.50%. The bond has a call feature that allows the issuer to redeem the bond at par in 10 years. The dollar price of this bond figured to its 20-year maturity is approximately 104¾. Should the bond be called after 10 years, you receive par for the bond, and based on your paying 104¾, the yield of your investment would be 8.29%, not 8.50%. But you were entitled to a 8.50% return on your investment based on the terms of your purchase. Therefore this callable bond must also have its price figured to the call date in 10 years. In effect, the presence of a 10-year par call possibility establishes 10 years as the possible maturity of the bond, and 10 years will be used for the bond calculations rather than the bond's 20-year stated maturity. If you are to receive 8.50% return to the 10-year call date established by the possibility of a call, the dollar price of the bond drops from 104¾ to approximately 103.32, and this lower price is the price of the transaction. If the bond is not called and goes to its final maturity in 20 years, the lower price of 103.32 would result in an increase of yield from 8.50% to 8.65%. Again, the pricing of a callable bond must insure that the purchaser gets at least the yield offered at the time of the transaction.

Current government regulations require that bond dealers provide information regarding bond calls on their sales confirmations. Sometimes the fact that the bonds are callable, or details about the call features, are hidden in the fine print of the confirmation. Before you make an investment in a callable bond, find out all aspects of the call features of the bond by asking your bond dealer the following questions:

1. What are all the possible types of call options that exist on the bonds, including extraordinary call options?

2. If the bonds are callable, when are they callable and at what price?

3. For a given dollar price, what is my yield to both the call date and to the maturity date?

One final warning about callable bonds: if a bond is selling at a premium and the bond can be called, assume the bond will indeed be called. Never believe someone trying to sell you a callable premium bond with a story of how the bond will not be called. No one can predict whether or not a bond will be called; if you assume it will be called in making your investment decision, you will not be hurt if the bonds are called. If you don't, you can be stung.

9

packaging
bonds

THE BOND FUNDS

Municipal bond funds were made available to individuals starting in 1961 when tax legislation was changed allowing a pass-
through of interest income from the fund's portfolio to investors
who held shares in the fund. Investing money and purchasing
securities through a fund is not a new concept; investment
trusts originated in Scotland in the 19th Century. Mutual funds
of equities became a popular method of investing in the stock
market during the bull markets of the 1950s, and it was a logical
evolution for bond funds to develop in the early 1960s. Recent
years have seen tremendous growth in the sale of municipal
bond funds as shown by Figure 9.1.

The easiest way to conceptualize a bond fund is to consider it
to be a mutual fund, but a bond fund contains fixed-income debt
obligations rather than common stock. Bond funds can hold various types of taxable and tax-exempt bonds. In this chapter, we
will discuss only tax-exempt bond funds. There are two major
types of municipal bond funds: the unit investment trust and the
open-end bond fund.

UNIT INVESTMENT TRUSTS

A unit investment trust is a form of closed-end bond fund. A
closed-end fund makes initial purchases of securities when the
fund is sold to investors; no additional buying or selling of securities is expected to take place within the fund after the initial
purchases are made. The unit investment trust is the most common type of municipal bond fund. When most investors purchase
municipal bond funds, they are investing in unit investment
trusts.

Municipal bonds are purchased and placed into a fund or trust
during a short period by a municipal bond firm called the sponsor or manager. After the bonds are purchased, the sponsor delivers the bonds to a bank that will act as the trustee for the

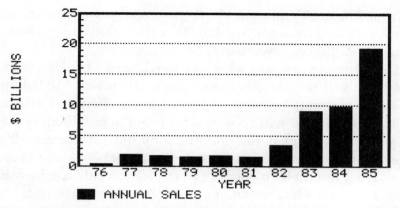

Figure 9.1 Bond fund sales. (Courtesy Investment Company Institute, Washington, D.C.)

fund. As the purchase of bonds for the fund is being finalized, the fund is sold to the investing public. The investor purchases a number of units in the fund; a unit typically represents $100 or $1000 par value of securities held in the unit investment trust. The sponsor owns the bonds from the time of purchase until the time the investor buys the units of the fund. During this time, the sponsor is exposed to changes in the value of the bonds held in the fund should the market value of the bonds fluctuate. For this reason, the sponsor will try to assemble a fund that is large enough to be a good source of profit and yet small enough to be sold quickly to investors. Approximately two to three weeks will pass from the start of purchasing blocks of bonds for the fund until the units are all sold to investors.

Any one sponsor may package hundreds of different funds. Each unit investment trust is a separate and distinct fund. Each starts at one point in time and ends after a number of years; in this respect, the unit investment trust resembles a bond itself.

A unit investment trust typically will contain anywhere from 20 to 40 different lots of municipal bonds with a total par value of from \$25 to \$75 million. For the investor, the minimum purchase will vary from \$500 to \$10,000 with \$1000 being the most common minimum investment.

The return you receive when you purchase units of the fund is fixed and will not vary. For example, if you invest \$10,000 in a newly issued unit investment trust that is offered at 100 and yielding 8.5%, you will receive a return of approximately 8.5% on your investment if you hold the fund until it matures. This fixed return of the fund is a second example of how a unit investment trust resembles a bond. Of course, if you paid a price other than 100, your yield would not be 8.50%. If the price were over 100, your yield would be less than 8.50%, and, if the price were under 100, the yield would be greater than 8.5%.

Bonds in a unit investment trust are bought and held to maturity. There are two exceptions where bonds would be sold before their maturity: first, if the sponsor thinks that it would be in the interest of the fund and its investors to sell any bonds because of their deteriorating quality, the trustee will do so. Second, if fund holders wish to sell their units and the sponsor can not resell these units to new investors, the trustee must liquidate bonds in the fund to raise the cash needed to redeem the units being sold. Looking at a unit investment trust from a practical viewpoint, the investor should assume that the bonds in the fund at the time of purchase will remain in the fund until either the bonds are called or mature. After the unit investment trust is brought to market, no new purchases of bonds may be made for the trust.

As interest is paid on the bonds held in the fund, the interest is held by the trustee bank for periodic distribution to the fund holders. Investors can choose to receive their interest on a monthly, quarterly, or semiannual basis. There will be a small reduction in overall return if you opt for monthly or quarterly distributions of interest due to the additional administrative costs involved.

Fund holders will receive a return of their principal investment from three different events occurring in the unit investment trust. First, as time passes, some of the bonds in the fund will probably be called. Second, at some point bonds will mature. Third, some bonds may be sold before their maturity. The principal received from the called, matured, or sold bonds is distributed by the trustee to the fund holder. Eventually the fund shrinks as fewer and fewer bonds remain in it; after the last bond is called or matures, the fund makes its final payment and goes out of existence. All principal must be distributed to the shareholders, as unit investment trusts do not make any additional bond purchases after the initial purchases that were made when the fund was established. Both the interest and principal payments that are distributed by the fund are subject to any tax considerations of the fund holder. The unit investment trust is a pass through vehicle and has no tax liabilities of its own.

OPEN-END MUNICIPAL BOND FUNDS

The main difference between the unit investment trust and the open-end fund is that the latter buys and sells municipal bonds on an ongoing basis. Bonds are bought and sold by the open-end fund to try to achieve a higher return on the bond portfolio. Decisions to buy or sell bonds are made by the fund's manager or investor advisor. Money can be periodically added to or withdrawn from an open-end fund. Additional money from investors coming into an open-end fund will allow it to grow as the manager purchases more bonds in the marketplace; if holders want to withdraw money, the manager either sells bonds from the fund to raise cash or uses new cash inflows to provide for redemptions. There is no distribution of principal to the fund investors; the only way principal is received by an investor is through the sale of an investor's holding of the fund. The ongoing buying and selling of municipal bonds by an open-end fund is similar to a mutual fund's activity in the stock market. A number of the larger open-end municipal bond funds are listed in the mutual funds tables in *The Wall Street Journal* and other major financial publications. Unlike unit investment trusts, open-end funds do not have a limited time to run; the open-end fund will exist as long as investors are willing to hold shares of the fund.

GENERAL MARKET FUNDS VERSUS STATE FUNDS

As investor acceptance of bond funds increased, a market developed for more specialized types of funds. At first, municipal bond funds were available that contained bonds from a variety of different states; these funds are called general market funds. The general market fund created a problem for an investor living in a state with a high income tax rate because the income received from this type of fund was subject to state income taxes. For example, if you live in California, the interest you receive from a general market bond fund is exempt from California income taxes only to the extent that the bonds in the fund are California municipals. If the fund had 5% of its portfolio invested in California securities, only 5% of the income would be exempt from California income taxes. State municipal bond funds evolved to give the investor exemption from federal, state, and local income taxes. You can invest in a municipal bond fund that will contain only bonds that are exempt from the income taxes imposed by a given state. These funds have become very popular with investors living in states with high income tax rates.

Because there are a variety of different state tax considerations, the holder of a general fund must know the percentage holdings of the fund in bonds of each state to determine if there is a tax liability for out-of-state bonds. Because of this requirement, at the end of each year, the general market bond fund provides the fund holder with a statement of the percentage of bonds held from each state for the preceding year.

The return on a state municipal bond fund tends to be less than the return on a general bond fund. In purchasing bonds for a fund, the sponsor will try to buy the highest yielding bonds within the fund's quality and maturity guidelines. However, bonds issued by states with high local income taxes will sell at higher prices and lower yields than the bonds issued by states with lower tax rates. Bonds issued by states with low tax rates will be concentrated in the general market funds, and bonds issued by states with high tax rates will find homes in the appropriate state municipal bond funds. Investors must analyze the return on a general market fund versus a state fund to see if the higher return from the general market fund compensates the purchasers for any potential liabilities they may have for state taxes.

INSURED BOND FUNDS

Insured bond funds have some form of insurance feature on the bonds held by the fund. The insured bond funds can be found in the form of both general market funds and state funds. If you invest in bond funds and are a conservative investor, insured bond funds are for you.

Bond insurance will pay any interest or principal payments that are due if a bond held in the fund were to default. The insurance payments are made by the insurer to the trustee bank and handled just as any interest or principal payment. If an investor holds an insured bond fund and one or more of the bonds in the fund defaults, the fund holder should see no difference in the income received from the fund, as the insurance company will make good any payments that are due.

There are two types of insured bond funds. One fund purchases bonds that are insured by a bond insurer. Each bond in the fund's portfolio has a separate and distinct insurance policy associated with it. If the sponsor had to sell a bond from the portfolio, the bond would be sold as an insured bond. The other type of insured fund has an insurance policy wrapped around all the bonds in the portfolio; this is the more common type of insured fund. When the sponsor is packaging the bond fund portfolio, the sponsor buys an insurance policy for all the bonds in the fund. The insurance policy covers all the bonds as long as the bonds are in the portfolio; however, individual bonds are not insured if the bonds have to be sold from the portfolio. For example, the sponsor purchases 25 lots of bonds that are rated "A" by Standard & Poor's to form the trust; the sponsor then buys an insurance policy covering all the bonds in the portfolio. With the insurance policy in place, Standard & Poor's gives the fund a "AAA" rating. The "AAA" rating is for the fund; the individual bonds within the fund retain their "A" rating. If the sponsor had to sell bonds from this fund, the bonds will receive a bid reflecting their individual "A" rating, which will be less than the value of the bonds with a "AAA" rating. As most investors in bond funds hold them as a source of long-term income and not as a trading vehicle, the problem of selling an uninsured lot of bonds from an insured fund is more a theoretical problem than practical one. But investors should be aware of the difference. The first type of insurance, that is, the insurance on each lot of bonds both in and out of the fund, is safer than the second type, the insurance wrap around. If you can purchase the first type at a similar return to the second, go for the safety of the direct insurance on each bond.

Insured bond funds have two additional investment considerations. First, if you are buying insured bond funds, realize that the quality of the fund is only as good as the quality of the insurer. In Chapter 11 we consider bond insurance. All aspects of the discussion of insurance for bonds applies to insurance for bond funds. Second, everything has its cost including the insurance for a bond fund. Investors pay the cost of the insurance by receiving a reduced yield on their investment in the fund; insurance will lower the return on a fund by approximately 30 basis points. Investors must decide if the extra safety feature of insurance compensates for the reduction in income.

MATURITY VARIATIONS

Most investors think of bond funds as vehicles for investing in long-term bonds. However, there are two other types of bond funds composed of tax-exempt securities with intermediate and short-term maturities.

Intermediate funds hold bonds so that the average life of the portfolio will be anywhere from three to 10 years in length as opposed to the 20- to 30-year average life of the long-term bond fund. The yield on intermediate funds will normally be less than the yield on long-term funds, but the market fluctuations of the fund's principal value will be less as interest rates move up and down.

The tax-exempt short-term funds have all the characteristics of the popular taxable money market funds; in fact they are often referred to as tax-free money market funds. These funds are valued at 100, hold short-term securities, have an average maturity of several months, and provide check writing privileges. They are designed more for the temporary holding of cash rather than for permanent investments. The tax exemption for this short-term fund arises from the securities that the fund holds. The portfolio will be comprised of state and municipal debt obligations with short-term maturities. In addition, the short-term funds invest in bonds with short-term put options, which allow the fund to redeem the bonds at 100 within a forthcoming short period. The "dividends" paid by the tax-exempt money market fund will have the same tax advantages for investors as would municipal bond interest. As you can imagine, the return on short-term funds will tend to be very low when compared with long-term investments. Tax-exempt money market funds are not available as insured funds; the very short-term nature of their holdings does not make insurance meaningful for these funds. There are a limited number of tax-exempt money market funds that are comprised of short-term securities issued by only one state; currently they are available for California, Connecticut, and New York. These funds allow the investor to avoid state and local income taxes.

COMBINATIONS AND PERMUTATIONS

Selecting a bond fund is like ordering from a menu in a Chinese restaurant; you first order something from column A and then something from column B. Figure 9.2 shows some of the combinations you can develop; choose one item from each column and find that particular type of fund that meets your investment objectives. For example, you could invest in a bond fund that is long term (column A), insured (column B), and exempt from a given state's taxes (column C). Maybe your needs call for an intermediate, uninsured, general market fund. Nearly all the combinations exist. Your bond dealer will gladly assist you in finding the fund that comes closest to your investment objective.

FIGURE 9.2.   Municipal Bond Fund Combinations

Column A: Maturity	Column B: Quality	Column C: Local Tax Consideration
Long-term	Insured	General market
Intermediate	Uninsured	State exempt
Short-term		

ADVANTAGES OF INVESTING IN TAX-EXEMPT FUNDS

No investment is perfect; each investment has both risks and rewards. Municipal bond funds are no exception. Bond funds are a product that is very highly advertised by the investment community, and the investor is often exposed to the rewards of bond funds without knowing their risks. There also are several major misconceptions concerning bond funds. The discussion of the pros and cons of bond funds in the remainder of this chapter will emphasis long-term unit investment trusts; however, the general concepts can be applied to all types of tax-exempt funds.

The primary advantages of bond funds include:

1. Diversification
2. Professional selection and credit monitoring
3. Portfolio services
4. Ease of buying and selling
5. Reinvestment options

When you invest in a bond fund, you are buying an interest in each of the bonds in the fund's portfolio. Each purchase of a bond fund represents a series of smaller purchases in each lot of bonds in the fund. It would be difficult for the average municipal bond investor to develop a portfolio as diversified as the portfolio of a bond fund. Diversification is a desirable objective for any investment program, and the bond funds provide excellent diversification. However, you should realize that diversification for a bond portfolio is not as important a factor as is diversification for a common stock portfolio. In a stock portfolio, stocks go up and down in price based upon what is happening to a particular industry or company. Bonds react differently. Bonds go up or down in value based upon changes in interest rates; rarely would one bond fluctuate in price independently from the overall bond market price movements. If you are investing in quality bonds, diversification is a much less important consideration for your portfolio than would be the case for a common stock portfolio. Moreover, if you invest in a state fund composed of municipal bonds issued from only one state, you lose the value of diversification to a great extent because all your eggs are in one state's basket. In fact, many of the state bond funds are described as being nondiversified in their offering prospectus.

If you choose a bond fund offered by a well-known sponsor,

you can assume that you will have professional selection of the bonds in the fund's portfolio. Publications like *Forbes* and *Barron's* have periodic issues and articles showing the results of various fund's management; these articles will give you a good indication of previous track records. Read the prospectus for the fund you are considering; find out what are the investment objectives of the fund and the parameters under which the fund will operate. Even if the bonds are chosen by the best of sponsors, if the types of bonds that can be included in the fund are not to your liking, avoid that particular fund. One of the problems of investing in a unit investment trust is that it is difficult to determine what bonds will be in the fund before making your investment. The time frame is so short between the purchase of the bonds and the sale of the fund's units that the investor is usually investing in a fund without knowing exactly what bonds are actually going to be in the fund. Reviewing previous unit investment funds of the same sponsor does not remedy this situation as each fund is a separate and distinct portfolio. What was contained in a previous fund has no bearing on what will be purchased for the new fund even if both have the same sponsor.

Municipal bonds held by the individual investor do require a certain amount of servicing. If the bonds are in coupon form, there is the security problem of handling the bond certificates and the bother of semiannual processing of coupons. If the bonds are registered, there is the need to see that interest checks are properly received. For all bonds, there are the problems associated with bonds being called and with collecting the proceeds from maturing certificates. All of these bond housekeeping services are handled by the trustee bank for the fund and for its investors. In addition, the fund holder receives periodic statements of the status of his account which simplifies investment record keeping.

For many investors, it is easier to buy or sell bond funds rather than municipal bonds. Bond funds allow investments to be made with a smaller initial purchase than would be required to buy a bond. Many bond funds allow an initial investment of

$1000, whereas the minimum bond purchase would be for a $5000 par value bond. You will receive a certificate of ownership after making an investment; Figure 9.3 shows a sample of a typical certificate. Of course, you can have these certificates held by your bond dealer. Once the investment is made in a fund, the investor can find the market bid price of the fund by a toll free call to the sponsor; finding the bid price of a bond can be a time-consuming procedure for the investor. Selling is simplified because the fund holders can liquidate part or all of their holdings by returning their certificate to the transfer agent or by instructing their broker of their intention of selling if the broker is holding the certificate. The price received at the time of sale will be the bid side market evaluation for the securities held in the fund. The seller has the comfort of knowing that the price received at the time of sale will be totally fair and honest. The evaluation of the bonds will be done by a professional, third-party evaluator; the bid will not be at the whim of one bond trader.

Lastly, many funds give the investor the option of automatically reinvesting interest income as it is received into the same or another tax-exempt fund. This simplifies the reinvesting process and allows investors to have their income compounding in a tax-exempt environment.

DISADVANTAGES OF BOND FUNDS

Now let's look at the other side of the ledger. Again we are concentrating on unit investment trusts for this discussion. The major disadvantages of bond funds are:

1. High costs
2. Lower yields
3. Maturity risks
4. Credit risks

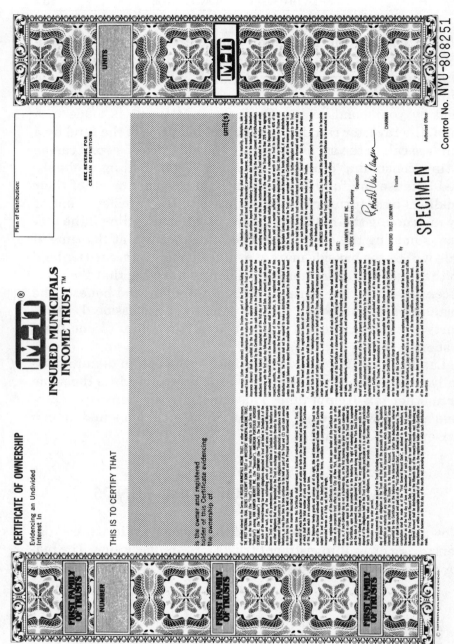

Figure 9.3   Bond fund certificate.

138

I am sure that you have seen the many ads in the newspapers and on television for tax-exempt bond funds. Entire pages of leading newspapers are filled with an advertisement for just one municipal bond fund. Ads for tax-exempt funds appear regularly on prime time television. These forms of advertising are obviously very costly, and the investor who purchases bond funds is the one who pays for the advertising. You may have noticed that stock brokers and bond salespeople encourage many investors to purchase bond funds. Because these sales representatives are paid on a commission basis, you should be a little leery of their enthusiasm for bond funds.

Let's examine just how much profit is incorporated into the bond fund by seeing how a typical fund is packaged and brought to market. The sponsor buys blocks of bonds in the marketplace. Because the sponsor is looking for larger blocks of $1 to $2 million of bonds with interest rates reflecting current market conditions so that the fund will have an offering price close to par, much of the fund's buying activity will be concentrated in the new issue market. The sponsor many times is also a bond dealer. As a dealer, the sponsor's firm is likely to be a member of the syndicate underwriting the same new issues that will appear in the bond fund. If the sponsors buy bonds for the fund through their own dealer activity, the dealer department of the sponsor can earn a profit on the initial sale of securities into the fund. This occurs because the sponsor's firm, as a dealer, obtains the bonds at a dealer's discount or concession, as the sponsor is a member of the underwriting syndicate. In turn, the bonds are sold to the fund at the higher public offering price. A concession for the general types of bonds found in many bond fund portfolios will be about $15 per $1000 par value of bond. For a $25 million bond fund, this would result in a profit of $375,000 for the dealer department of the sponsor's firm if all the bonds in a fund were obtained by this method. But wait, for the profit has only started to accumulate on the transaction.

After the bonds have been purchased by the fund, the bonds

typically are marked up anywhere from 3.5 to 5.0% from their purchase price. Let's assume the markup is 4.5%; this means an increase in price of $45 per $1000. If the investor makes a $10,000 purchase, the gross profit in the transaction would be $450. The 4.5% markup will be split, with the broker or dealer who sold you the fund receiving about 3% and the remaining 1.5% going to the sponsor. For a $25,000,000 fund, a 4.5% markup translates into $1,125,000 of gross profit potential. This profit is in addition to the profit that the sponsor may have made at the time the bonds were initially purchased for the fund. The spread of 3.5 to 5% is probably the highest profit margin associated with any class of transactions involving municipal securities. Because profit greases our economic system, you can see why bond funds are a highly advertised and heavily pushed investment product.

The profit on any one unit of a bond fund can be obtained by the municipal securities industry several times over. If you buy a newly issued unit, there is the initial markup. If you sell the unit before it matures, you will receive a price reflecting the bid side of the market at the time of sale. The unit you sold will be offered in turn to another investor at the offered side of the market, which means a second markup. For example, let's say you purchase a unit of a new fund at 100. Time passes and you want to sell the unit. Interest rates have declined since you made your purchase so that the price of bonds has increased. Due to market conditions, the bid side of the market for the bonds in the fund has increased to 102 and you have made a two-point capital gain. This unit will now be offered in the secondary market for unit investment trusts, which operates in a similar manner to the secondary market for municipal bonds. When a new buyer purchases what had been your unit, the price to the new buyer will be the offered side of the market for the unit which includes another markup. The new purchaser will pay approximately 106 to 107 for what had been your unit. Every time the unit trades, it generates another markup. The markup for bond funds in the secondary market is normally greater than the markup for bond funds at the time of their initial offering, thereby making the re-sale of unit investment trusts extremely profitable for the dealer

The markup and sales charges make municipal bond funds an extremely poor short-term investment. You should purchase this type of investment for a long-term holding rather than a short-term investment.

Remember the price–yield relationship for bonds: if one goes up, the other goes down. If there are high costs associated with investing in bond funds, these costs result in a reduction in the yield on your investment. Purchasing bonds through the fund vehicle results in lower returns than if you purchased compara-ble bonds themselves. This follows from the markup that occurs in selling the fund. For example, assume you can invest in an in-sured bond fund yielding 8%. If you can buy an insured bond with a similar maturity to the average maturity of the bonds in the fund, protected by the same insurer, and yielding 8.50%, why not invest in the one insured bond rather than in the fund? Both the single bond and the fund are insured by the same in-surer so that the quality of both is the same; if the maturity of both are similar, take the extra 50 basis points of yield. Remem-ber you will receive that extra 50 basis points of tax-exempt yield each year you hold the bond. Over time, that adds up to be a very meaningful amount. For example, 50 basis points a year on a 20-year, $100,000 investment, means an additional $10,000 of tax-exempt income.

Bond funds that are advertised as "no load" do not have a one time front end markup; the profit for these funds is hidden else-where. "No load" funds charge annual management or advisory fees of upwards to 1% each and every year. I have seen a well-advertised municipal bond fund with annual management fees and expenses of nearly 2% per year. This fund was yielding ap-proximately 8% a year. In this case, expenses were devouring

25% of the total income of the fund. Don't be so gullible to think that a sales representative will try to sell you an extensively advertised product without the presence of substantial profit. There is no such thing as a bond fund without high profit, just as there is no such thing as a free lunch.

Unit investment trusts normally are composed on very long-term bonds. The sponsor markets the funds on the yield of the portfolio; the larger the yield, the greater the appeal to the purchaser. Because there are numerous funds competing for the investor's dollar, the yield offered by a fund is an important element in its advertising and marketing. Bonds of the longest maturity provide the highest yield, but in most municipal market conditions, the longest maturity of bonds may not represent the best overall buy for the investor. Let's assume that 15-year bonds are yielding 8% and that 30-year bonds are yielding 8.25%. The fund purchases the 30-year bonds to get the extra yield, but extending the maturity from 15 to 30 years—the risk factor—is not compensated by a mere 25 basis points extra return—the reward factor. When you purchase a bond fund, you are buying a share interest in a portfolio of long-term bonds; your investment is a long-term investment.

The goal of having the highest possible yields to offer potential investors can lead the sponsor to stretch the quality of the bonds in the portfolio to the absolute limit. Most securities in the funds have an "A" rating from either Moody's or Standard & Poor's. Bonds in the fund will tend to be of the lowest allowable quality within the fund's guidelines because lower rated bonds return a higher yield. I have seen many cases where an investor would not invest in a particular type of tax-exempt bond, say a hospital revenue bond, yet this same investor will invest in a bond fund that is stuffed with the same type of bonds the investor would not purchase directly. Again, remember that bond funds are pass-through conduits; when you invest in the fund, you are investing in the bonds held by the fund.

INVESTOR MISCONCEPTIONS ABOUT BOND FUNDS

There are several misconceptions about bond funds in the minds of many investors. These misconceptions arise from two sources. First, advertising strongly emphasizes positive features while giving little mention of the risks. Second, overzealous security salespeople like to offer an easily retailed investment product that has a high profit margin attached to it. The main misconceptions are:

1. Bond funds are liquid, whereas bonds are not.
2. Bond funds' principal is guaranteed.
3. Bond funds are safer than bonds.

Liquidity is the ease with which a security can be sold and converted into cash. If you want to sell a municipal bond, you should receive the money from the sale in five business days, which is the normal settlement time for the sale of a security. The sale of the bond should take place on the same day that you give instructions to your dealer to sell the bonds. There will be rare occasions when it may take several days to sell the bonds due to the small lot size, the unusual nature of the bonds in question, or poor bond market conditions. When you sell units of a bond fund, if you hold the certificate, you must mail the certificate to the transfer agent with instructions to sell part or all of your holdings. Only when the transfer agent receives the certificate will the sale of the bond fund units occur. You will receive the price per unit based on the next evaluation of the fund. This will be either the day the transfer agent receives the certificate or the next business day. In turn the transfer agent mails you a proceeds check so the check will arrive five business days after the sale of the units. By adding the time required for mailings and processing, you can see that there is no time advantage in liquidating a bond fund over selling a bond; in fact, it may take you more time to get money out of a fund than from the sale of a municipal bond itself.

Many investors have told me that their bond funds are "guaranteed." By guaranteed, these investors think that they will receive the same money they paid for the fund at any time should the fund be sold. This is obviously not the case. Somehow the features of an insured bond fund are erroneously conceived as constituting a guarantee of the principal value of the fund units. When a bond fund is insured, the insurance pays principal and interest when due on a defaulted bond held in the fund. Insurance does not guarantee protection from market fluctuations. Investors purchasing a tax-exempt fund during times of low interest rates can receive a nasty shock when they try to sell their investment in an atmosphere of higher interest rates.

Bond funds are only as "safe" as the bonds held in the fund. If an investor held four lots of $25,000 par value of good quality, "A" rated bonds, or if an investor has $100,000 invested in a bond fund of similar maturities and quality, the safety factor of each portfolio is basically the same. If you sell a bond fund, the proceeds of the sale will be based on the current market value of the bonds held in the portfolio. This value will be more or less than the price you paid for the bonds. The chances are remote that you will get exactly the same price that you paid for the bond fund should you sell it. Of course, you will get the face value of the bonds in the fund if you wait until all the bonds eventually mature, but remember, 25 to 30 years can be a long wait.

ARE FUNDS GOOD OR BAD?

Whether investing in a long-term unit investment trust is a good or bad investment depends on the investor, and the investor's needs and objectives. Funds are excellent investment vehicles for some investors and poor ones for others. How do you fit into this picture? Here are several questions to ask yourself. Each question you answer "yes" is a point for investing in a fund; a "no" response is a point for investing directly in a bond.

1. When you make an investment in the municipal market, do you normally have *less than* $25,000 to invest?

2. Do you find record keeping, interest collecting and reinvesting, and the housekeeping associated with bonds to be a time-consuming and annoying chore?

3. Do you feel uncomfortable making an investment selection of a particular bond because you don't know enough about the bond itself?

4. Do you want to have a diversified portfolio *and* are you willing to give up some yield to get this diversification?

5. Do you want to invest mainly in *long-term* bonds that constitute most unit investment trusts?

The more questions you answered "yes," the more attractive you will find long-term bond funds. These answers, plus the discussions in this chapter of how the funds operate and their relative advantages and disadvantages, should help you decide if funds should form a part of your portfolio. If they should be in your investment holdings, your bond dealer will be more than willing to provide you with a prospectus for the type of fund that meets your investment objectives. And remember—as the bond funds tell you in their advertisements—read the prospectus carefully before investing or sending money.

short-term
municipal
securities

Investors purchasing tax-exempt securities usually consider only the longer term municipal bond market, in which bonds can have maturities ranging upwards to 40 years. There is another important sector of the tax-exempt market for investors seeking a short-term investment for their money. This chapter will discuss tax-exempt securities that have maturities of one year or less. We will consider their relative advantages and disadvantages, and the role that short-term municipal securities should play in your portfolio.

The volume of short-term securities sold by states and municipalities has not shown the dynamic growth pattern displayed by municipal bonds. Figure 10.1 shows the pattern of note sales during the past 20 years. The spikes that occurred in the early 1980s were caused by states and municipalities increasing their short-term borrowing to avoid locking themselves into the high rates that were prevalent at that time in the long-term market. As interest rates have fallen in recent years, note financing has decreased in favor of long-term bond sales.

TAX-EXEMPT NOTES

The most common form of short-term municipal securities are tax-exempt notes. These notes are usually issued in bearer form, pay all their interest at maturity, are noncallable, and have specific maturity dates. A sample of a typical municipal note is shown in Figure 10.2. There are three different types of notes currently available for purchase by investors: bond anticipation notes, tax anticipation notes, and revenue anticipation notes.

Assume that a community wants to build a new school that will be financed by the sale of long-term municipal bonds. Bond anticipation notes can be sold to raise the funds needed to start the school's construction. The issuing municipality might sell notes at the early stages of construction because the final cost of the school may not be known or because the issuer believes that

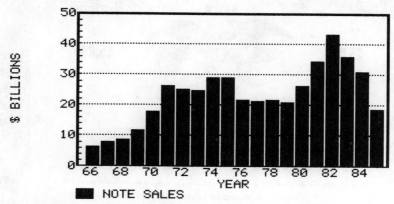

Figure 10.1   Note sales. (Courtesy *The Bond Buyer,*)

market conditions are not favorable for a sale of long-term bonds. The bond anticipation notes (BANs) will be redeemed with the proceeds of the bond sale; the long-term bonds in turn will provide the permanent financing for the school.

A good way to look at the relationship between short-term bond anticipation notes and long-term bonds would be to consider the financing of the construction of a new home. The builder obtains a short-term loan to finance the construction of the house. When the house is sold by the builder, the purchaser obtains a mortgage on the house. The proceeds from the mortgage allow the builder to repay the outstanding short-term loan. In this situation, the builder's short-term borrowing is analogous to the bond anticipation note, and the mortgage is analogous to the long-term bonds.

What happens if the community can not sell long-term bonds to redeem the bond anticipation notes? Most states allow a municipality the option of refinancing note issues several times; this refinancing is called "rolling over" the notes. In our example of the new school, if the community had previously sold a one-year note, a new one-year note could have been sold at the maturity of the first note. The second note would provide the

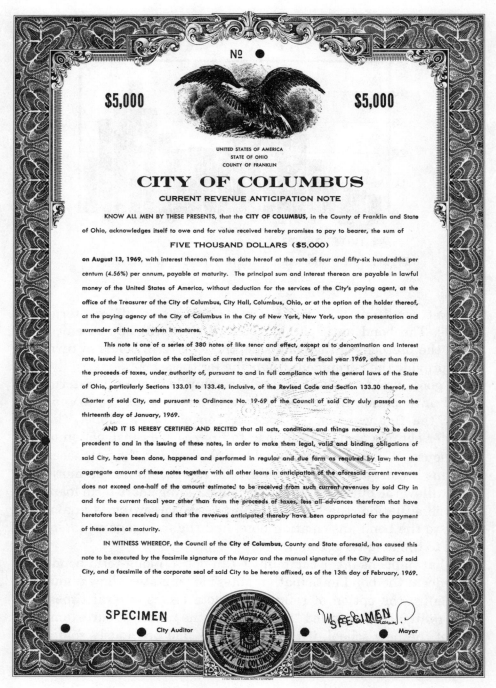

№ ●

$5,000 $5,000

UNITED STATES OF AMERICA
STATE OF OHIO
COUNTY OF FRANKLIN

CITY OF COLUMBUS
CURRENT REVENUE ANTICIPATION NOTE

KNOW ALL MEN BY THESE PRESENTS, that the **CITY OF COLUMBUS**, in the County of Franklin and State of Ohio, acknowledges itself to owe and for value received hereby promises to pay to bearer, the sum of

FIVE THOUSAND DOLLARS ($5,000)

on August 13, 1969, with interest thereon from the date hereof at the rate of four and fifty-six hundredths per centum (4.56%) per annum, payable at maturity. The principal sum and interest thereon are payable in lawful money of the United States of America, without deduction for the services of the City's paying agent, at the office of the Treasurer of the City of Columbus, City Hall, Columbus, Ohio, or at the option of the holder thereof, at the paying agency of the City of Columbus in the City of New York, New York, upon the presentation and surrender of this note when it matures.

This note is one of a series of 380 notes of like tenor and effect, except as to denomination and interest rate, issued in anticipation of the collection of current revenues in and for the fiscal year 1969, other than from the proceeds of taxes, under authority of, pursuant to and in full compliance with the general laws of the State of Ohio, particularly Sections 133.01 to 133.48, inclusive, of the Revised Code and Section 133.30 thereof, the Charter of said City, and pursuant to Ordinance No. 19-69 of the Council of said City duly passed on the thirteenth day of January, 1969.

AND IT IS HEREBY CERTIFIED AND RECITED that all acts, conditions and things necessary to be done precedent to and in the issuing of these notes, in order to make them legal, valid and binding obligations of said City, have been done, happened and performed in regular and due form as required by law; that the aggregate amount of these notes together with all other loans in anticipation of the aforesaid current revenues does not exceed one-half of the amount estimated to be received from such current revenues by said City in and for the current fiscal year other than from the proceeds of taxes, less all advances therefrom that have heretofore been received; and that the revenues anticipated thereby have been appropriated for the payment of these notes at maturity.

IN WITNESS WHEREOF, the Council of the **City of Columbus**, County and State aforesaid, has caused this note to be executed by the facsimile signature of the Mayor and the manual signature of the City Auditor of said City, and a facsimile of the corporate seal of said City to be hereto affixed, as of the 13th day of February, 1969.

SPECIMEN
● City Auditor

● Mayor

Figure 10.2   Municipal note, City of Columbus.

funds to redeem the first note. Typically, there are limitations on the number of times that notes may be rolled over. Even though the sale of long-term bonds is the intended source of re- payment for bond anticipation notes, these notes usually are also general obligations of the issuing community. Because they are general obligations, the total taxing power of the community can be used for their payment. The pledge of both the proceeds of a bond sale and the community's taxing power makes these notes a form of double-barreled municipal obligation.

Municipalities receive many of their tax receipts in a limited number of installments during the course of a year; for example, property taxes are normally collected only once or twice each year. However, the need for cash on the part of the community is on an ongoing basis. Tax anticipation notes (TANs) are sold to provide the cash needed by municipalities between tax collec- tions. The forthcoming tax receipts are pledged to redeem the tax anticipation notes. In addition, these securities are usually general obligations of the municipality.

Revenue anticipation notes (RANs) are issued by a commu- nity when funds are expected to be received from another gov- ernmental source. For example, a town might sell revenue antic- ipation notes in the expectation of state aid payments or of revenue from a federal grant program. The revenue anticipation notes are backed by the pledge of the expected payments, and, like the other anticipatory notes, typically are general obliga- tions of the issuer.

As most issues of BANs, TANs, and RANs are general obliga- tions of the issuer, these securities should be analyzed in the same fashion as you would analyze a general obligation bond of the same issuer.

Municipalities sell notes at competitive sales to municipal bond dealers who in turn distribute the notes to investors. The bid that the dealer makes on a note issue becomes the interest rate or coupon that the notes will bear for their duration. If you purchase newly issued notes from a dealer, you can expect to pay a slight premium for the notes. The dealer most likely purchased the notes at par from the municipality and must mark the notes to a premium in order to make a profit on the transaction. For example, assume that a dealer purchases a nine-month note issue with a bid of 6% for the notes. The 6% bid of the dealer becomes the interest rate on the notes. Because the dealer bid par for the notes, the dealer must sell the notes at some price over par to make a profit. The dealer may offer the notes to yield a 5.50% return to the investor; this would result in a price to the buyer of 100.31, or a premium of $3.10 per $1000 note.

In addition to notes that are general obligations of an issuer, notes are sold by authorities that do not have any taxing power. These notes, issued by authorities that can pledge only their stream of revenues, should not be confused with revenue anticipation notes which have the security backing of general taxing power. Notes of authorities that do not have taxing power should be analyzed in the same fashion as revenue bonds of the issuing authority.

On occasion, municipal authorities will issue notes with maturities of several years. These securities, although called notes, have the same investment characteristics as bonds: they are issued in registered form, pay interest every six months, and may have call features. Investors should treat these notes as if they were bonds.

You should be aware of one additional type of tax-exempt note: project notes. Project notes were sold by various local housing authorities to provide short-term financing for housing-related activities throughout the country. Because the housing authorities are municipal entities, the notes were tax exempt. Project notes were sold under a contractual agreement with the U.S. Department of Housing and Urban Development; this contract provides the guarantee of the United States for the payment of the principal and interest on the notes. Project notes resembled tax-free treasury bills and represented the highest quality short-term municipal note investment. The sale of project notes was stopped by the federal government in August 1984, and project notes are no longer available in the marketplace. However, there is always the possibility that the project note program may be restarted in the future.

TAX-EXEMPT DEMAND NOTES

There are two types of tax-exempt demand notes: variable rate notes and floating rate notes. Both types of notes have fluctuating interest rates and give investors the option of redeeming their investment on very short notice.

The interest rate on a variable rate note is adjusted on a periodic basis to reflect some well-publicized base rate. For example, the interest rate may be set each week as a percentage of the weekly auction rate on treasury bills. Let's say that a variable rate note pays 80% of the weekly six-month treasury bill rate. At a sale of treasury bills, if the six-month rate is 7%, the rate for the variable rate note will be 5.60% (80% of 7%) for the first week. At the next auction, if the six-month treasury bill rate is 7.5%, the rate on the variable rate note will be 6% (80% of 7.5%) for the second week. The interest on the variable rate note will change each week and the new rate will be in effect until the next treasury bill auction. Any well-known base rate can be used to determine the rate on the variable rate note. Once a rate is established, it will determine the interest rate for some limited period, which could be a week, a month, or a quarter of a year. Weekly variable rate demand notes are the most common.

Floating rate notes, or "floaters," have interest rates that are adjusted constantly and automatically as their designated base rate changes. The time frame that any given interest rate will apply to the floating rate note is totally variable and will be set by the base rate and changes occurring to the base rate.

Both types of demand notes have a put feature that allows the investor to redeem the note at par by notifying the issuer of the intention of the investor to demand payment. The actual sale of the note normally takes place five business days after the holder of the note gives an indication that the note will be put back to the issuer. If one investor sells the demand note, the dealer involved with placing the note tries to locate a new investor who will purchase the note. If a new investor can not be found, the demand note must be redeemed by the issuer. To insure that funds will be available should a demand note have to be redeemed, these notes are backed by letters of credit issued by major domestic and foreign banks. The letters of credit permit the issuer to borrow funds that are needed to redeem the notes if new investors can not be found.

Because these notes have a very short term put feature which allows the holder to receive par for the note, the market value of the note will always be approximately par. This feature makes demand notes an ideal investment for short-term tax-exempt money market funds, which will be discussed later in this chapter.

PUT BONDS

Long-term municipal bonds with put features convert long-term investments into short-term investments. A put bond is one that gives the holder the option of redeeming the bond at par at some specific dates before the bond's maturity. A put bond is the opposite of a callable bond; whereas the callable bond allows the issuer to redeem the bond from the holder at the issuer's option, the put bond allows the holder to redeem the bond and collect the bond's principal from the issuing municipality at the holder's option.

Put bonds are issued with long-term maturities. After a period of time, the put option becomes effective. For example, a municipality may issue a bond with a 25-year maturity; after the first five years of the bond, the put becomes effective and the bond can be put each year on some given date, say each July 1st. In this example, after the initial five-year period, the investor can sell the bond back to the municipality on any July 1st and receive par for the bond. The put bond represents a short-term tax-exempt investment if there is one year or less to the next put option date.

There are two important features of put bonds that can create problems for investors. First, the put date, like July 1st in the above example, is the date that the issuer redeems the bond. But if you want to exercise your option to put your bond, you will be required to take action several months before the put date. In the example, if July 1st is the put date, you might have to notify the issuer or the issuer's agent in writing of your intention of putting the bonds several months before July 1st, let's assume between March 1st and March 31st. During March, you would have to deliver the bonds to be put along with your written notice of intention. Once delivered, the decision to redeem the bonds through the put option is usually not revocable. You must know all the details of the procedures to be followed to properly put the bonds: the time of giving notice of intention, who receives the notice, and who receives the bonds. This information is contained in the bond's prospectus. In some cases, it is printed on the bond itself. If you invest in a bond with a put feature, obtain this information at the time you make the investment and retain the information as part of your permanent investment records.

What happens if you miss the period for giving your notice of intention? This creates the second problem with put bonds. If your bond has an annual put which allows you to tender the bond once a year, the worst thing that can happen is that you are locked into your investment for another year. If you have to sell your bonds in the secondary market, the bid on the bonds will reflect the next put option date as the maturity date, and therefore the bid should be close to 100. The financial trap opens from the fact that some put bonds have only one put option or a put option only every five years. If you miss the put by not fulfilling some technicality, your short-term investment is instantly converted into a long-term one. Let's assume our 25-year bond example has a one time put option for next July 1st; this one time put gives the investor only one option to redeem the bond. You are holding this bond as a short-term investment because of the option and for planning purposes, you consider next July 1st to be the maturity date. However, you fail to notify the issuer of your intention to put the bonds during the month of March. On April 1st, your bond has lost its put option and has magically become a bond with 20 years left to maturity. As the dollar value of bonds with short-term put options normally is much higher than the dollar value of long-term bonds with the same rate of interest, the market value of your bond plummets on April 1st, even though April 1st is still three months before the July 1st put date. For example, if the yield spread between one-year municipal securities and 20-year municipal securities is 250 basis points, missing the put will cause the value of your bonds to drop about 25 points, or $250 per $1000 bond. Obviously, this is a severe penalty for missing the put date. Because of the inherent danger in these types of bonds, you should avoid put bonds unless the bonds have an annual put option.

A bond with a one-year put option should yield more than a one-year note. The extra yield compensates the investor for the mechanical procedures that complicate the put bonds when they are held by investors. Be extremely careful if you purchase a put bond; you must know in detail all the procedures that are necessary to exercise the put option. If you don't, this could be a case in which the municipal market will "put it to you."

There are also municipal bonds with mandatory put options. This bond represents another form of short-term tax-exempt security. A mandatory put option requires the investor to tender bonds on the put date. After the mandatory put date, the bond does not pay any interest. A new bond normally will be issued after the mandatory put takes place, and investors have the option either of converting into the new bond issue at its new rate of interest or of taking their funds out of the security investment. Because mandatory puts do not give any discretion to the investor, the put date is really the bond's maturity date for all practical purposes.

TAX-EXEMPT COMMERCIAL PAPER

Some major municipalities issue tax-exempt commercial paper that has similar investment characteristics to commercial paper sold by large industrial and financial companies. Tax-exempt commercial paper is issued in $100,000 multiples; the large denominations of tax-exempt commercial paper place this type of security out of reach of the majority of individual municipal investors. Letters of credit are used as backing if new investors can not be found to purchase maturing commercial paper. The use of letters of credit in conjunction with tax-exempt commercial paper is similar to the use of letters of credit with municipal demand notes.

TAX-EXEMPT MONEY MARKET FUNDS

All of the types of short-term securities that are discussed in this chapter can be found in the portfolios of the tax-exempt money market funds. In fact, the marketplace has produced municipal demand notes and commercial paper primarily to meet the short-term liquidity needs of the tax-exempt money market funds. These short-term funds, which were discussed in Chapter 9, are not considered by many purchasers to be an investment as such, but rather as a place to hold cash until the cash is needed for a more permanent investment or for some other purpose.

For the investor in a high tax bracket, the tax-exempt money market fund normally represents a better vehicle for highly liquid funds than would a taxable money market fund. Compare the return you receive from the tax-exempt money market funds with the after tax return you receive from treasury bills or other short-term taxable investments. Tax-free money market funds have many of the characteristics of the taxable money market funds, including check writing privileges. *The Wall Street Journal* and other major newspapers periodically list the current returns available from the major tax-exempt money market funds.

The units in a tax-exempt money market fund are always carried at a price of approximately $1.00 per unit. The securities are evaluated on the basis of their amortized cost, which assumes that the interest income on each security in the portfolio is constantly accruing until it matures. Using amortized cost disregards any change in market value while the notes are held by the fund; this is considered to be a prudent approach to their evaluation due to the high quality and short-term nature of the holdings in the tax-exempt money market funds.

RATING SHORT-TERM MUNICIPAL SECURITIES

Both Moody's and Standard & Poor's rate municipal notes and other short-term municipal securities. As an investor, you should be as concerned about the quality of a short-term investment as you would be about the quality of a long-term one. Many times investors become lax about quality considerations when investing in short-term tax-exempt paper on the false rationale that because the investment is short term in nature it must be safe. In recent years, several of the major financial difficulties that developed in the municipal market arose from careless note issuing by municipalities and equally careless short-term investing by buyers. The New York City financial crisis in the mid-1970s was a prime example of municipal notes helping to create severe investment problems.

Either Moody's or Standard & Poor's short-term municipal rating can be used as a guide in making your investment decision, but do not make your decision solely on a rating without additional knowledge of the issuing municipality.

Moody's assigns a "Moody's Investment Grade" (MIG) rating to notes ranging from a high of "MIG 1" to a low of "MIG 4." Standard & Poor's assigns three different rating categories to municipal notes and to tax-exempt demand notes with "SP-1+" denoting the highest grade and "SP-3" the lowest. Both Moody's and Standard & Poor's note ratings are defined in detail in Appendix A.

You should only consider investing in notes that are rated either "MIG 1" or "MIG 2" by Moody's or "SP-1+" or "SP-1" by Standard & Poor's. Investors erroneously equate the various grades of note ratings to the various grades of bond ratings. For example, some investors consider a note issue rated "MIG 1" or "SP-1" to be the equivalent of a bond rated "Aaa" or "AAA." This is not necessarily the case as the criteria used in assigning note ratings are different from the criteria used in assigning bond ratings. This can be demonstrated by the relative ratings currently assigned to the short-term and long-term debt of New York City: Moody's rates the notes of New York City "MIG 1," simultaneously rating New York City's bonds "Baa 1."

Many note issues are not rated. If the note does not have a rating, use the bond rating of the same issuer as a guide to the quality of the municipal note. For example, if the general obligation bonds of a community are rated "A," the nonrated note issue of the same community is often referred to as having "an underlying 'A' rating." You can safely use the bond rating as a proxy for the note rating if the notes themselves are not rated.

ADVANTAGES AND DISADVANTAGES OF SHORT-TERM PAPER

Considering all the types of short-term tax-exempt securities as one general class of investments, what are their relative advantages and disadvantages?

The primary advantage is liquidity. If a need to have access to cash and the smallest possible fluctuation of principal is important for a portion of your portfolio, consider short-term tax-exempts. If you think that interest rates will be increasing, invest in short-term securities until you are comfortable with the level of longer term rates. If interest rates do increase, the market value of all fixed-income investments decline. However, the decline will be much less for short-term maturities than for long term. A short-term security will return your capital quickly; at that time, you may have the opportunity to reinvest your funds in a higher long-term rate environment.

In addition, if you see a definite need for funds in the near future, short-term notes may be the best investment alternative. For example, if you know you are going to need money for taxes next April 15th, consider investing in municipal notes with maturities around that date.

The primary disadvantage of investing in short-term tax-exempt securities is their low return. These securities give the investor about the lowest return of any investment. Of course, you must analyze your return on an after tax basis and then compare the return with other short-term alternatives. In addition, the short-term nature of these securities deprives you of any potential capital gain that may be associated with declining interest rates. If you think interest rates will decline, you should not have excess capital invested in short-term securities.

11

security
enhancements

The investor looks to the issuer of a state or municipal bond as the source of the funds for the repayment of interest and principal on the debt. The taxing power or revenue generating ability of the issuer will provide the wherewithal to meet debt service. If investors are seeking additional bond security beyond the security of the issuing municipality itself, they should consider municipal bonds with security enhancements. A security enhancement is some source aside from the issuer of the bonds that provides funds to pay debt service if the issuer cannot meet interest and principal payments. Enhancements are provided by third parties, such as insurance companies, or by the deposit of marketable securities or cash with a trustee by the issuer of the bonds. If you are the type of investor who likes to wear a belt plus suspenders to insure that your financial assets are secure, enhancements on municipal bonds are for you.

Bonds with security enhancements became popular with investors starting in the mid-1970s. In early 1975, the New York State Urban Development Corporation defaulted on a municipal note issue. This episode was soon followed by New York City's well-publicized financial crisis. The magnitude of the New York City crisis was so large that it spread a cloud of uncertainty not only over the bonds of New York City but also over the bonds of New York State itself and over all the authorities and municipalities in New York State. These events also made investors think seriously about the security backing of all municipal bonds, be they general obligations or revenues. New York City bonds were one of the most widely held municipal securities by individual investors in the country so that the New York City crisis caused tax-exempt bond investors to question the ability of municipalities to provide debt service, including debt service for the heretofore sacrosanct general obligation bonds. Maybe, just maybe, the bondholders' claim to the general tax receipts of a municipality did not rank first and come before the need to pay the salaries of teachers, firefighters, and the police.

INSURED BONDS

Municipal bonds can be insured by individual or groups of commercial insurers. Insured tax-exempt bonds have shown remarkable growth since their introduction in the mid-1970s. In 1973, approximately $1 *million* of newly issued municipal bonds were insured. The number of newly issued municipal bonds with insurance that were brought to market in 1985 alone had increased to an incredible $47 *billion*. During the past 10 years, insured bonds sold in the new issue market have increased from an insignificant amount to nearly 25% of all long-term bonds issued by states and municipalities. This tremendous growth is an example of market reaction to the needs of the individual tax-exempt investor for increased security for municipal bond investments.

How does municipal bond insurance work? There are two major ways that insured bonds are made available to investors: direct insurance on an issue of bonds and insurance of unit investment trusts.

Direct insurance is provided on a bond issue or some maturity segment of an issue when the bonds are sold in the new issue market. The initial cost of the insurance will be paid either by the bond issuer or by the bond underwriters. If the underwriter pays the cost of the insurance, the cost is factored into the underwriters' bidding strategy.

With most insured municipal bonds, a one-time premium is paid for the bonds to be insured when the issue is brought to market. However, some bond issues are insured with the municipality paying an annual premium based on the par value of the outstanding bonds. Once an insurance policy is issued, it is not cancelable even if the municipality does not pay the annual insurance premium.

The cost of the premium will be a function of the quality of the issuer, the maturity structure of the bonds, the interest rate on

the bonds, and the size of the issue. As with any insurance transaction, the lower the risk that is perceived by the insurance company, the lower will be the premium. The insurer of a large bond
issue or of several issues of the same municipality often will use
reinsurers to reduce the total liability exposure to any one issuer. Municipal bond issuers also can use reinsurers to shift part
of the risk associated with bonds already insured so as to have
the ability to increase the number of newly issued bonds that
can be insured.

No matter what mechanics are used in insuring a municipal
bond issue, the bond investor is the party who ultimately pays
the cost of the insurance. The cost of the insurance premium is a
direct cost in the underwriting process, and this cost results in a
reduction in the yield on the bonds that will be received by the
investor. The reduction in yield is the real cost of the insurance,
and this cost is always borne by the investor. If an "A" rated municipal bond is insured, its yield will be reduced anywhere from
20 to 40 basis points. The reduction in return will vary as market conditions change and as the spreads between medium grade
bonds and prime grade bonds widen and narrow. As the yield
spreads between insured and uninsured bonds narrow, the insured bond becomes a better investment because the reduction
in yield, which is the real cost of the insurance, is reduced. As
the yield spread widens, insured bonds become more expensive
to buy than uninsured bonds.

When a bond is insured, what exactly is insured? What happens if there is a default on the part of the municipality that has
issued insured bonds? This is an area of confusion on the part of
many investors who have insured tax-exempt bonds in their
portfolios. Bond insurance provides the timely payment of interest and principal on the bond if the issuer fails to make interest
or principal payment for any reason. Insurance does not provide
for the accelerated payment of the principal of the bond if the issuer defaults on an interest payment. Bond insurance will provide the funds to redeem the bonds at their maturity only if the

issuer does not have the funds to repay the principal of the bond at that time. For example, suppose you buy a 20-year insured bond. All goes well for the first 10 years; for some reason, after the 10th year the issuer cannot meet the interest payments. As each semiannual interest payment date arrives, the insurer pays the required interest payment to the paying agent; the paying agent in turn pays the investor. The investor receives the interest payment as if the issuer of the bond were still paying interest. The municipality that issued the tax-exempt bonds now has a liability to repay the insurance company for any payments that the insurer has made to bondholders.

At maturity, a similar transaction would take place. If the municipal issuer defaults on the repayment of principal, the insurer provides the funds to redeem the bonds to the paying agent, who in turn makes payment to the bondholder.

If you own a defaulted insured bond with the insurer providing the debt service payments, you could sell the bond in the secondary market in the same fashion as you would sell any other municipal bond. In theory, neither the market nor the investor should be concerned with the source of the funds used for debt service as long as the interest and principal payments are being made. However, an insured bond that is in default, even if the insurance company is paying the debt service, will probably trade at a discount due to the stigma attached to the fact that the municipality has defaulted.

In addition to a bond issue itself being insured, insurance policies can be obtained for bonds in a municipal unit investment trust. Many sponsors of unit investment trusts offer insured tax-exempt funds whereby all the bonds held in the fund carry insurance protection. The insurance may arise from the bonds held in the fund being insured themselves or from an insurance policy guaranteeing all bonds in the fund as long as they are held in the fund. In Chapter 9 there is a more detailed description of insurance as it applies to securities held in bond funds.

What are the tax implications of receiving municipal bond interest from an insurance company rather than from a state or municipality? The Internal Revenue Service has ruled that interest payments on insured municipal bonds received from an insurance company will be treated for tax purposes as if the interest payments were received directly from the municipality that originally issued the bond. Do not fear that the receipt of interest from the insurer will change the tax status of the payment.

WHO ARE THE INSURERS?

There are several major insurers who provide municipal bond insurance for both bond issues and bond funds. Most of the municipal bond insurers represent a consortium of owners consisting of casualty insurance companies, commercial banks, financial companies, and stock brokerage firms. The first insurer to offer municipal bond insurance was the American Municipal Bond Assurance Company; the largest insurer of tax-exempt securities today is the Municipal Bond Insurance Association.

The major insurers of municipal bonds include:

1. Municipal Bond Insurance Association (MBIA) is composed of five leading casualty insurance companies: Aetna Casualty and Surety Company, Fireman's Fund Insurance Company, The Travelers Indemnity Company, Aetna Insurance Company, and The Continental Insurance Company. MBIA is the largest insurer of municipal bonds and notes; MBIA insurance policies have backed almost 4000 different municipal bond and note issues with a par value of nearly $44 billion. To date, there has never been a default on any issue insured by MBIA. Bonds insured by MBIA are given a "Aaa" rating by Moody's and a "AAA" rating by Standard & Poor's.

2. The American Municipal Bond Assurance Company, or AMBAC, has Citicorp as its majority owner. The minority owners include Xerox Corporation, Stephen Inc., and several officers of AMBAC. AMBAC has insured over 5000 issues of tax-exempt bonds with a par value of approximately $30 billion. Standard & Poor's grants a "AAA" rating to AMBAC insured bonds; however, Moody's does not give any improved rating status to bonds carrying AMBAC insurance. This rating split results in unusual situations in which an insured bond will have the top "AAA" rating from Standard & Poor's while being rated a more modest "A" or even "Baa" by Moody's. Unlike MBIA, AMBAC insurance has been put to the test. Several AMBAC-insured issues have defaulted. In addition, some unit investment trusts insured by AMBAC held bonds of the Washington Public Power Supply System #4 and #5 when these issues went into default. AMBAC is currently making the interest payments on these defaulted bonds.

3. The third major insurer in the Financial Guaranty Insurance Company (FGIC). There are a number of participants in FGIC including General Electric Credit Corporation, General Re Corporation, J. P. Morgan & Co., Lumbermans Mutual Casualty Company, Merrill Lynch & Co., Shearson Lehman/American Express, and G. L. Friedman. FGIC has insured close to 1000 municipal bond issues with a par value in excess of $11 billion. Like MBIA, FGIC insured bonds receive the coveted top bond rating of "Aaa" from Moody's and "AAA" from Standard & Poor's.

MBIA, AMBAC, and FGIC account for about 90% of all the municipal bonds that have been insured. Two other insurers account for most of the remaining 10%: Bond Investor's Guaranty and Industrial Indemnity Company. Bond Investor's Guaranty insurance earns a "Aaa" from Moody's and a "AAA" from Standard & Poor's. Industrial Indemnity Company's insurance does

not have the highest rating from either of the two major rating
agencies.

PROS AND CONS OF INSURED BONDS

What are the advantages and disadvantages of insured bonds in
your portfolio? If you are a risk avoider, insured bonds are for
you. These bonds have two separate layers of security: the issuer
of the bonds and the insurer of the bonds. The pledge of the insurer to make payments of interest and principal in the event of
a default is unconditional. The insurers do not enter into a policy
to insure a bond issue until after they have done an extensive
credit review of the issuing municipality. Only bond issues that
the insurers think will pay their debt service will be insured.
For example, more than 6000 different municipal bond issues
have been submitted to MBIA for insurance since MBIA started
insuring bonds in 1974; of this total 82% were approved but only
55% of these issues were actually sold with MBIA insurance.
The review by the bond insurers gives additional comfort to the
investor who is looking for a well-secured investment.

Because a bond issue must pass credit review before the insurer will issue an insurance policy, these issues represent interesting investment opportunities for the individual investor.
When a rating agency such as Moody's or Standard & Poor's reviews a bond to assign a bond rating, there is no financial risk on
the part of the rating agency if the rating agency makes an error
in judging the bond issue. For example, if Moody's rates a bond
issue "A" and in the future the issue is downgraded, Moody's
suffers no financial loss as the market value of the bond drops
due to the downgrade. However, if the insurer reviews an issue
and insures the bonds, the insurer will sustain a definite financial loss should the bonds default. Needless to say, bond analysts
working for the insurance company will do very thorough and
practical research on a municipality before agreeing to insure

an issue because of the possibility of financial loss in the event of a default. Given this extensive review on the part of the insurers, if a municipality can come to market with an insured issue, why not invest in an *uninsured* bond of the same municipality? The fact that the municipality meets the investment criteria of the insurer for a new bond issue is a good indication of the overall investment strength of the issuer. Why not invest in the lower rated, higher yielding, outstanding, *uninsured* bonds of a municipality whose new issue is being marketed with insurance? If you do invest in the uninsured bonds, make sure it has a claim to taxes or revenues equal to that of the insured bond.

Another advantage of insured bonds involves those insured bonds that have the highest rating from both Moody's and Standard & Poor's. The "Aaa" rating given a bond due to its insurance is probably less likely to be downgraded in the future than is the "Aaa" rating on a bond without insurance because financial problems with the municipality are more likely than financial problems with the top-rated bond insurers.

There is only one disadvantage to insured bonds: lower yield on your investment. The fact that insurance premiums are ultimately paid by the investor lowers the yield on insured bonds. However, insured bonds normally do yield a higher return than bonds rated "Aaa" on their own merits. Insured bonds typically return a yield that reflects yields on "Aa" bonds even though the insured bonds are rated "Aaa." For the risk averse investor, insured bonds represent excellent value.

There are differences, however, between the various municipal bond insurers. All insurers are not created equal. The individual investor in tax-exempt securities is not in a position to analyze the various reserve backings and state regulations that result in some bond insurers being stronger than others. There is a good rule of thumb that you can follow: if you limit your purchases of insured bonds to those bonds that are rated "Aaa" by Moody's *and* "AAA" by Standard & Poor's, you will be investing in the strongest category of insured bonds.

One last consideration while discussing the pros and cons of insured bonds should be given to municipal bonds backed by pools of insured mortgages. These bonds do not have direct insurance but are supported by assets that are insured. For example, a local housing authority issues a revenue bond that is secured by a pool of single-family mortgages. Each mortgage in the pool is insured by the Federal Housing Administration or by the Veterans Administration. If there is a default on any mortgage in the pool, either the Federal Housing Administration or the Veterans Administration advances the funds needed to satisfy the mortgage. Bondholders could experience a slight delay in receiving their interest or principal payments, but in time the payments will be received. The insurance is on the mortgages in the pool; there is no guarantee on the municipal bonds themselves by either the Federal Housing Administration or the Veterans Administration. Commercial mortgage insurers offer similar programs to insure mortgage pools. However, I recommend that you limit your investments to the insurance programs of the two federal government agencies and avoid the programs of commercial insurers. In addition, look for a "Aa" or a "AA" rating on these bonds; this rating will give you assurance that the bond issue is properly structured to comply with the programs of the government agencies.

LETTERS OF CREDIT

The second major category of security enhancement is provided through letters of credit. A letter of credit is issued by a bank in favor of the municipality, whereby the bank is obliged to lend funds to the municipality to pay interest and principal on a particular bond issue. The best way to describe this procedure is to follow a municipal issue through the letter of credit process. A municipality is planning the sale of a bond issue; the municipality negotiates with a bank to have a letter of credit drawn in favor of the the bond issue. The municipality pays a fee of about

1% of the total par value of the issue to have the letter of credit drawn. The bank will issue the letter of credit only if the bank is satisfied as to the financial strength of the municipality and the viability of the bond issue in question. Each year that the letter of credit is outstanding, the municipality pays the bank a fee based upon the par value of the bonds still outstanding. Under the terms of the letter of credit agreement, if the issuer of the bonds does not have funds available to pay interest or principal, the bank must lend the issuer the funds to make debt service payments. The funds borrowed from the bank can be used only for payments due the bondholders; in fact, the borrowed funds normally are sent directly to the trustee or paying agent of the bond issue and not to the municipality that is borrowing the funds. The letter of credit creates a form of a backstop for the bonds in case the municipality finds itself in a financial bind.

You should be aware of four important limitations of letters of credit as they apply to municipal bond investments. First, a letter of credit does not result in a bank guaranteeing a bond issue. Investors often think that the presence of a letter of credit represents an unconditional guarantee on the part of the bank to repay the bonds if the issuer defaults. The letter of credit only obliges the bank to lend funds if the municipality is complying with all of the terms of the letter of credit. Second, the bank is not unconditionally obliged to lend funds to pay the debt service. If the bond issuer violates any part of the letter of credit agreement between the issuer and the bank, the bank is no longer obliged to lend the funds. For example, the letter of credit agreement might require the municipality to keep the facility that is producing the revenue to repay the bonds insured against fire. If the facility is not insured and burns down, no revenue is generated to pay the bonds and the bank is not obliged to lend funds for debt service because fire insurance was not in place. Third, many banks have been aggressively providing letters of credit arrangements due to the fee income that the letters of credit generate for the banks. Some bank analysts and regulators consider that letters of credit—a form of off-balance sheet financing for the banks—have grown much too quickly in recent years. To many observers, the growth of letters of credit represents another form of overextension on the part of some banks, similar to the overextension in lending to third world countries. Municipal bond investors should always remember that the letter of credit is only as strong as the bank issuing it. Lastly, many foreign banks have entered the United States letter of credit market by making letters of credit available to states and municipalities selling tax-exempt bonds. A letter of credit issued by a foreign bank introduces additional elements of risk and uncertainty. The financial statements of foreign banks provide less information about the financial condition of the foreign banks than do comparable statements of United States banks. The investor also runs the risk of currency controls being implemented, which could restrict the borrowing against a letter of credit. In addition, the knowledge foreign banks have about the financial activities of United States municipalities is questionable. It always seems very strange to see a Japanese bank issuing a letter of credit for a municipal bond issue rather than a local domestic bank: can one really believe that Japanese bankers are in a better position than the local municipality's bankers to judge the quality of a municipal bond issue?

If you invest in a tax-exempt issue accompanied by a letter of credit, you should limit yourself to those letters of credit issued by strong, highly rated, domestic banks. Find out what ratings the bank issuing the letter of credit has received from Moody's and Standard & Poor's. Avoid letters of credit issued by foreign banks and by United States banks that are having problems of overextension in foreign and energy-related loans.

COLLATERALIZED BONDS

The third category of bonds with enhancements are collateralized bonds. A municipal bond issue is collateralized if, when the bonds are initially sold to investors, the bonds are secured by a portfolio of marketable securities in addition to the pledge of the issuing municipality to provide debt service. Many collateralized municipal bond issues are associated with college, university, and hospital revenue bond issues. For example, a university sells a $20 million bond issue; simultaneously the university delivers to a trustee bank $20 million of marketable securities from its endowment funds. The securities could be Treasury bonds, corporate bonds, common stock, or any combination of these securities. The trustee bank will hold the securities in escrow as long as the university's bond issue is outstanding. If the interest or principal are not paid in a timely fashion by the university, the trustee bank will liquidate securities in the escrow portfolio and use the proceeds from the sale of the securities to pay interest and principal due to the bondholders.

Look for a "Aaa" or a "AAA" rating on any collateralized bonds you might be considering for your portfolio. This rating will assure you that the collateralization agreement is properly drawn. All collateralized bonds are not rated "Aaa" or "AAA" because some collateralization agreements allow the issuer to substitute lower quality securities in the portfolio or to remove securities from the portfolio before the maturity of the collateralized issue.

ESCROWED AND PREREFUNDED BONDS

The last category of enhanced bonds—escrowed and prerefunded—are similar to collateralized bonds in that these bonds use a portfolio of securities to secure the bonds in addition to the pledge of the bond issuer. The main difference is one of timing: collateralized bonds are secured by a portfolio of securities from their initial sale date, whereas escrowed and prerefunded bonds are secured at some point between their initial offering and their maturity.

Most escrowed and prerefunded bonds result from refundings of existing bond issues. For example, assume that a municipality had an issue of 12% bonds outstanding; interest rates dropped, and this same municipality could sell bonds with an interest cost of 8%. A new issue of bonds was sold to raise funds which were invested in a portfolio of United States Treasury bonds. The interest payments for the old bonds will be paid from the interest received from the portfolio of Treasury bonds. This transaction reduced the municipality's overall interest costs and typically resulted in the older bonds receiving a "Aaa" or "AAA" rating. The older bonds are now said to be escrowed, or escrowed to maturity. The older issue will not be called on a call date, should there by a call option on the bonds, but rather the bonds will pay interest until the final maturity of the issue. The funds needed to pay the principal at maturity are provided by the maturing Treasury bonds.

A prerefunded bond is similar to an escrowed bond, except that the older bonds will be called on some specified call date before the maturity of the bond. The call date for prerefunded bonds becomes the new maturity date because the bonds will definitely be called on the indicated call date. In our example, assume that the 12% bonds mature in the year 2012, but they are callable in 1996 at a price of 102. If the sale of the new 8% bonds resulted in funds being deposited with a trustee to call the bonds in 1996 at 102, the older issue is prerefunded.

Information about the price and availability of escrowed and prerefunded bonds can be found in a separate section in the back of each day's *The Blue List*.

Both escrowed and prerefunded bonds are riskless investments as regards to credit because the money is, literally, in the bank to provide their remaining debt service. Of course, as with all bonds regardless of quality, you can expect fluctuations in market value due to changes in interest rates.

HIGHLIGHTS CONCERNING ENHANCED BONDS

1. Insured bonds represent excellent value for the investor seeking a safe haven. However, if you are seeking extra

safety, don't gamble with the credit of the insurer; invest only in insured bonds rated "Aaa" by Moody's and "AAA" by Standard & Poor's.

2. Only invest in letter of credit arrangements provided by financially strong domestic banks.

3. Collateralized, escrowed, and prerefunded issues have no credit risk. Look for a "Aaa" rating on these bonds; this will give you the assurance that a rating agency has reviewed the collateralization, escrow, or prerefunding documents.

12

portfolio

management

Probably the most difficult thing that individual investors must do before investing in municipal bonds is establish parameters and guidelines for their portfolios. Investors would not call their stockbrokers and say that they wanted to buy "stock"; investors would have a particular company or industry in mind, and then working with their stockbroker, arrive at an investment decision. All too often, however, investors call their municipal bond dealer and purchase whatever tax-exempt bonds the dealer is offering. The portfolio that results has no direction, is composed of too many line items of odd lots of bonds, and does not dovetail into the overall investment objectives of the purchaser. Before investing in a municipal security, there are five parameters that you must consider: maturity of the security, risk factors, state tax considerations, portfolio diversification, and the dollar price of the bonds. After these five parameters have been considered, the investor should find a tax-exempt security that matches these parameters as closely as possible. Portfolio management also calls for consideration of a number of different lots of bonds in your portfolio, the size of each lot of bonds, and the use of bond swapping programs.

MATURITIES

Because municipal securities can be purchased with maturities ranging from several days to several decades, the investor can choose a maturity date that returns principal at some desirable point in the future. If you are seeking to maximize income, you will tend toward investing in longer term bonds. Yield curve analysis discussed in Chapter 3 shows you how to select the highest current return on your investment without an excessive extension of maturity to achieve the best risk–reward combination. On the other hand, if liquidity and avoiding market fluctuations in your principal value are your prime objectives, consider shorter term municipal securities.

Most investors will find themselves taking a compromise position when considering maturities for their portfolio. They will invest in varying maturities or have some percentage of their holdings in short-term maturities and some in longer term. The most important factor for you to think about is the maturity of an investment you are making and relate this maturity to your investment objectives and your other assets.

The best way to demonstrate how maturity factors should be applied to municipal portfolios is to look at some typical investors as they make decisions regarding a tax-exempt investment.

1. Mrs. Able's primary business is real estate. She wants to invest extra cash in municipals to gain tax-exempt income. However, she also wants to be able to have money readily available if an attractive real estate transaction should develop. Mrs. Able has been keeping her extra funds in the local bank's money market account because of her primary desire to have good accessibility to her money without any fluctuation in principal value. Mrs. Able should consider a short-term tax-exempt investment. Suggestions would include a tax-exempt money market fund, municipal notes with maturities of six months or less, municipal demand notes, or bonds with short-term put options. By establishing a short-term maturity as the primary objective for her portfolio, Mrs. Able can receive tax-free income and still have the liquidity she needs for her real estate transactions.

2. Mr. Baker has made some substantial profit in the stock market this year; he knows that he will have to make heavy tax payments over the coming months. Mr. Baker should consider municipal notes or short-term bonds that will mature close to the time of his tax payments. As the short-term securities mature, he will have the cash available to meet his tax payments.

3. Mr. and Mrs. Charlie have two children. The Charlies have money to invest, but they are concerned about financing the children's college education. It would be easy to determine what years in the future will require funds for each child's college expenses and purchase tax-exempt securities to mature in those years.

4. Mr. Delta is 10 years away from retirement. He knows that when he retires, his income situation will change and he will find himself in a lower tax bracket. Mr. Delta should invest in 10-year tax-exempts. This will give him the advantage of tax-exempt income while he is in a high tax bracket. It will also return the principal to him around retirement. After retirement, Mr. Delta can make investments based on his new tax situation or use his principal to buy his retirement dreamhouse in Arizona. Here again some factor aside from investing—planning for retirement in this case—establishes the maturity objective of the investment.

5. Mr. and Mrs. Fox are quite wealthy. They look to their extensive investment portfolio as their main source of income. The Foxes are not unduly concerned if the market value of their portfolio fluctuates as long as the income stream is maintained. They are fortunate enough to receive more money from their investments than they need to support their life style and find themselves reinvesting some of the income generated by their portfolio. The Fox's surely can invest in longer term bonds to maximize tax-exempt income because they do not look to the principal of their bond portfolio as a source of liquidity.

6. Mrs. Golf wants both a good income stream and periodic returns of principal from her portfolio. By investing in bonds maturing each year for the next 10 years, she reaches her objective. The maturity distribution of her portfolio resembles a flight of stairs, with some bonds coming due each

year for the next 10 years. As one of the lots of bonds matures, Mrs. Golf determines if she should invest the proceeds in another 10-year bond to keep the same maturity structure or if she should use the money for a different purpose. By having some bonds coming due each year, this investor also hedges herself against interest rate fluctuations.

Many investors will find a number of different maturity needs which are accommodated by their municipal bond portfolio. This will result in a mixture of maturities. But you should avoid a haphazard purchase of various maturities without any sense of investment objective. A random mixture of maturities usually indicates a lack of portfolio management and poor investment planning.

RISK FACTORS

Every investment has some element of risk. If you do nothing with your money and keep it in a safe deposit box or under the mattress, you run the risk of inflation slowly eroding the value of your money. Traditionally, there have been three major types of risks involved with purchasing municipal securities: credit risk, market risk, and inflation risk. A new risk factor that I call political risk has recently become very important.

Credit risk deals with the intrinsic value of the particular bond you purchase. Credit risk is measured by bond quality; the lower the quality of the bond, the higher the credit risk, and the higher the quality, the lower the risk. If you apply the general principles of this book, know the bond rating, and purchase bonds from a reputable dealer, credit risk should not be a problem. From a credit risk viewpoint, municipal securities are the second safest class of investments; only bonds of the U.S. Treasury are considered to be of higher credit quality.

Using Moody's and Standard & Poor's bond ratings are the most practical way for the individual investor to determine bond quality and potential credit risk. These ratings are defined in Appendix A. Obviously, the better the rating, the lower the credit risk. Let me give you some guidelines about municipal bond ratings that you should follow:

1. *Never* invest in bonds rated below "Baa" or "BBB." These represent the lowest ratings that are considered to be investment grade; bonds with lower ratings are speculative and should be avoided.

2. *Never* invest in nonrated bonds. The absence of a rating removes a very important support from the investment decision. Furthermore, many bonds without a bond rating are deliberately not rated because the issuer or underwriter does not want the bonds to have a low, speculative rating.

3. If the bond is rated by only one of the two major rating agencies, reduce the one rating that is available by one notch for your investment planning purposes. For example, if Standard & Poor's rates a bond "AA" and Moody's does not rate the bond, consider the bond to have an "A" rating for your investment planning purposes.

4. In most cases, both of the rating agencies will assign the same rating to a bond issue. If the rating agencies disagree on a bond's quality and assign different ratings, use the lower rating in planning your investments. If Moody's rates an issue "Aa" and Standard & Poor's assigns the same issue an "A," use the "A" rating in formulating your investment decision.

5. For most individual investors, a rating of "A" from both rating agencies will be an indication of more than sufficient investment strength. You do not have to invest only in the highest rated bonds because these bonds return lower yields to investors.

6. A bond rating is just one factor in making a bond investment. Don't use the bond rating as an excuse for not having sufficient knowledge about the municipal bonds you are considering buying.

The most important risk you face when investing in municipal securities is market risk. All fixed income securities, regardless of their quality, are subject to market risk. Market risk is a function of interest rate movement. If interest rates go up, the market value of bonds—all bonds, both high quality and low quality—goes down; if interest rates go down, the value of bonds goes up.

Many municipal bond investors are concerned with preservation of the principal value of their portfolio and want to avoid downside market risk. If avoiding market risk is one of your objectives, invest in short-term or intermediate-term bonds rather than long term. With short-term or intermediate-term bonds, if interest rates rise, the change in principal will be less than would be the case with long-term municipals. The longer the maturity of a bond, the greater the change in the dollar value for any given change in interest rates.

Assume interest rates change by 25 basis points or one-quarter of 1% in all maturities; for example, rates change from 8% to either 7.75% or 8.25%. If you hold a five-year bond, the price change would be approximately $10.00 per $1000 par value of bond, whereas the change for a 15-year bond will be a little more than $21.00 for the same change in interest rates. If interest rates move by 100 basis points, the market value of a five-year bond will change by about $40, while the market value of a 15-year bond will change by about $80. A 100 basis point movement is not a great change considering the volatility of interest rates that has occurred in recent years. Figure 12.1 shows the change in dollar value for a $1000 bond for various maturities for both a 25 and a 100 basis point change in interest rates. The change in the market value of bonds will be inverse to

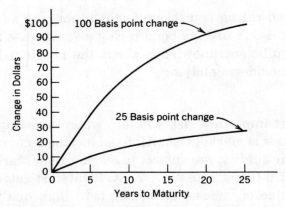

Figure 12.1 Changes in dollars for changes in basis points.

the change in interest rates. If interest rates increase, the value of bonds decreases and the market value of your portfolio drops. If interest rates decline, the value of bonds rises and the market value of your portfolio increases.

You should not be unduly concerned about the change in your portfolio's market value if the change occurs due to rising and falling interest rates. Let's compare common stocks and municipal bonds. If a stock falls in market value, it usually reflects changing earnings or some other factor that is inherent to the stock itself. If a municipal bond declines in market value, the most likely reason is increasing interest rates. The difference between the decline of the stock and the bond is that the bond will return to its par value as it approaches maturity, whereas the stock may never return to its higher valuation. For example, Avon common stock was selling at one time for $135 a share; at the time of this writing, it is selling for $32. Xerox stock has sold as high as $160 a share and now the stock is at $51. If you invested in these well-known companies at their record highs, the value of your investment may never return to your purchase price. If you purchase a bond at par and interest rates rise, the market value of your bond declines. At maturity, however, the bond will be worth par and receiving par at maturity is what you had anticipated at the time you made your bond investment.

If the price of a stock rises, the stock may be able to retain the advance and even rise further from the new level. If declining interest rates send the market value of a municipal bond to a premium, the premium will eventually disappear as the bond approaches maturity. In the long run, all bonds are worth 100: no more, no less. I suggest that you be less concerned about changes in market valuation of your bond portfolio than you are about similar changes in any common stock you might own. But if fluctuation of principal is a factor you want to minimize in managing your portfolio, avoid long-term bonds in favor of short-term or intermediate-term bonds. In most market conditions, the return you receive from intermediate-term bonds, say in the 10- to 15-year range, is not much different than the return you receive in the 25-year range.

The next major risk associated with investing in municipal bonds involves the changing value of the dollar or the inflation risk. Municipal bonds are fixed-income securities. For the vast majority of municipal bonds, the interest rate is established when the bond is issued and it will not fluctuate. During this century there have only been a few short times of high inflation when the decline of the purchasing power of the dollar exceeded the returns available from newly issued tax-exempt bonds. During most of this century, the return on municipal bonds has been extremely attractive for the investor in the higher tax brackets, even when inflationary factors were taken into consideration.

Some people who should invest in municipal bonds because of their tax bracket avoid tax exempts because of the inflation risk. These investors reason that $10,000 invested in municipal bonds 20 years ago is worth much less than the $10,000 returned when the bond matures. This is obvious. However, this reasoning overlooks what has happened to the bonds during the 20-year period. Assume the $10,000 bonds in question had a 7% coupon. Each year for the 20 years, $700 of tax-exempt income was generated. This cash flow could be reinvested or spent by the holder. If all the interest receipts—$14,000—had been reinvested, the total stream of returns at maturity from the initial investment would be the $10,000 from the principal of the bond, the $14,000 of tax-free income, plux the earnings of the $14,000 if it were reinvested. If the interest were reinvested at 7%—the same rate as on the bond—the reinvested interest would generate $15,000 more of interest through compounding. In this case the initial investment of $10,000 would result in a potential total return of about $40,000. If the interest rate used in the example were changed from a conservative 7% to 9%, the final figure goes from approximately $40,000 to $58,000.

The last risk factor is political risk. This is the risk that the government will take some action to reduce the value of your municipal holdings or tax the income you receive from municipal bonds. The Tax Reform Bill of 1986 demonstrates this risk. For the first time, the federal government is applying a direct tax on municipal bond income. Although the burden of this tax falls only on a small percentage of individuals who must pay an alternative minimum tax on nonessential municipal bonds, a precedent has been established for taxing "tax-exempt" bond income.

Let's consider the various risk factors in managing the municipal portfolios of several typical tax-exempt investors.

1. The Hotels are very conservative investors. They are very uncomfortable with any speculative elements in their investment portfolio. These investors should only consider higher rated bonds, insured bonds, and bonds backed by letters of credit from leading domestic banks. The bonds in their portfolio should have a maximum maturity of five years, with the portfolio staggered so that some bonds come due each year.

2. Mr. India is a typical municipal investor. He wants a good quality portfolio and high returns with little fluctuation of

principal. Mr. India should consider bonds with a "A" rating which will give him assurance of the basic credit worthiness of the bonds. This investor can get a good return with lower market risk if he analyzes yield curves to see where the "elbow" of the yield curve is located. At this maturity, he will receive a favorable return from his bonds without unduly extending maturities.

3. Mrs. Juliette has some money for investment speculation and she is considering speculating in tax exempts. My advice to her would be to seek some other market for speculation. If you speculate in municipals by purchasing very low quality bonds and if all goes well, at maturity you receive the face value of the bond. Your "winnings" in the bond market are always limited by the par value of the bond. If you speculate in the stock market and all goes well, you have the possibility of increasing your principal multifold. In theory, there is no limit as to the amount of the potential advance in the price of the common stock. The limitation of upside principal appreciation of bonds does not make the municipal market a good arena for speculation for the individual investor. You should look at tax-exempt bonds as investments and as sources of income, not as speculations.

STATE TAX CONSIDERATIONS

People invest in municipal bonds primarily to earn tax-free income. The more layers of taxations that are avoided, the greater the tax-free income. This brings state tax considerations into play as part of the management of your portfolio. We discussed state taxes in Chapter 7. Let's consider state taxes as they impact portfolio management.

If you live in a state with high income taxes, it would be good portfolio management to invest in bonds that are free of that state's income tax. This objective is well known by most municipal bond investors. Sometimes, however, trying to avoid state taxes can result in a poorer overall return on your portfolio, even taking possible liability for state taxes into consideration. Let's look at some examples of how these state tax considerations help, and hinder portfolio management.

1. Mr. Mike lives in New Jersey where there is a modest state income tax; the maximum rate is 3.5%. Mr. Mike invests in New Jersey municipal bonds to avoid the New Jersey tax. He does not realize that the yields on out-of-state bonds of comparable quality and maturity may yield more than the ones issued within his state. Mr. Mike should consider investing in bonds outside his state if the extra yield that can be obtained will more than compensate him for his tax liability to New Jersey. The municipal bond market is really a series of submarkets for the bonds of different states and municipalities. Many times, one state's bonds are offering more attractive yields than another state due to heavy supply considerations. Don't be afraid to invest outside your state if the extra yield you receive covers the tax liability to your state. If you do invest outside your own state, you also gain the element of portfolio diversification.

2. The Novembers live in New York State which has a very high state income tax. They have correctly invested in New York municipals to avoid the heavy state tax. Mr. November is retiring and the Novembers are moving to Florida. Florida has no state income tax. These investors should sell their New York bonds. These bonds have a premium price built into them due to their exemption from New York State taxes; this premium is no longer of value to the Novembers after they leave New York. By selling their New York holdings and buying bonds of other states, the Novembers will increase their tax-exempt income and

simultaneously diversify their portfolio. This constitutes a type of bond swap which is discussed in detail later in this chapter.

PORTFOLIO DIVERSIFICATION

Although diversification in managing a municipal bond portfolio is not as important a consideration as would be the case for a common stock portfolio, it should be one of your objectives. There still is truth to the old proverb "Don't put all your eggs in one basket." With municipal bonds, you should try to achieve diversification from a geographic viewpoint and also from the viewpoint of the type of economic activity supporting the bonds in your portfolio.

Whenever possible, your portfolio should contain bonds from a variety of different states. This can be difficult to achieve due to state tax considerations, but it still should be one of your objectives. In the mid-1970s the New York City financial crisis adversely impacted all the outstanding bonds issued by all the municipalities in New York State. The decline in oil prices in the mid-1980s put market pressure on the bonds issued by the oil-producing states. If you had to sell New York municipals in 1976 or Oklahoma municipals in 1986, their value would be depressed when compared with other times.

When considering geographic diversification, one factor that the California investor should consider is the possibility of earthquakes. If a community or a project suffered severe damage due to an earthquake, where would the resources be found to pay debt service? If you are purchasing California municipals, consider looking for bonds that have earthquake insurance coverage or that are covered by bond insurance.

The second aspect of diversification involves the economic activity supporting the bonds. Here diversification is easily obtained without sacrificing any loss of local tax benefits. Analyze your portfolio from the viewpoint of its backing. Where does the money come from to pay interest and principal? What percentage is general obligation and what percentage is revenue? Within the revenue category, avoid a large portion of bonds associated with any one form of economic activity. A heavy concentration of bonds backed by hospitals, power plants, or any other single category of revenues should be avoided. Spread the risk by diversifying your portfolio among several different categories of revenue bonds.

PREMIUM VERSUS DISCOUNT BONDS

From the viewpoint of portfolio management the dollar price of the bond—premium or discount—has advantages and disadvantages depending on your investment objectives.

Premium bonds have the advantage of high current tax-exempt cash flow; if current income is an objective, premium bonds should be considered for your portfolio. Don't think that a bond priced at a premium means that the bond is overpriced. The premium pricing on a municipal bond does not represent some type of excessive markup, but rather it reflects the higher interest rate of the bond. However, the higher dollar price associated with premium bonds many times discourages their purchase by investors. This reluctance to invest in premium bonds can work to your advantage. Many times premium bonds offer a higher yield to maturity or yield to the call date that can be obtained from bonds priced closer to par. For example, if the market offering for a new 15-year bond is 8%, a premium bond with the same maturity and quality may be offered to yield 8.25% due to the high dollar price of the premium. Go for the extra yield to maturity. It's yield to maturity that counts, not simplicity of pricing at the time you make your purchase.

There are, however, four disadvantages to premium bonds. First, these bonds have large coupons, and if they are callable, the higher the coupon, the more likely the possibility of a call. Many investors who purchased long-term tax-exempt bonds during the high interest rate period of the early 1980s will be saddened to see many of these bonds called by the issuing municipality at the earliest opportunity. It is easy to protect yourself against a call if you purchase premium bonds that are not callable. The second disadvantage results from the decline in the market value of the bond as it approaches maturity or a call date. Every premium bond, regardless of how large the premium, will be worth par at some point in the future. It is always difficult psychologically for investors to see the diminution of their investment as premium bonds approach maturity. Third, the amortization of municipal bond premium is not a capital loss and has no tax benefits. The gain in value due to the appreciation to par for a discount bond is taxed, whereas amortization of bond premium doesn't create a tax loss. This is a classic example of "heads the investor loses, tails the tax collector wins." Lastly, if the price of bonds is rising due to falling interest rates, the price advance of premium bonds will be less than the price advance of discount bonds. For example, assume there are two bonds whose market values are 90 and 110 in today's market; the values of 90 and 110 are due to the coupon each bond bears. Interest rates decline; the price of the bond originally at 90 rises to 100. The premium bond does not advance from 110 to 120; it does not match the 10-point increase of the discount bond. The premium bond will advance to approximately 117 or 118. This dampening of the advance of the price of the premium bond is due to its call possibilities and investor reluctance to paying high dollar prices for premium bonds.

Before making an investment in a premium bond, you must know if the bond is callable and the terms and conditions under which it can be called. Insist that the bond dealer show on the purchase confirmation the date and price of the first possible call. In Chapter 8, we discussed the need to know the yield to maturity and the yield to call if you are investing in a premium bond. Do not be content with knowing the current yield as current yield is not an accurate measurement of investment return on a premium bond.

Discount bonds, like premium bonds, have both advantages and disadvantages. The advantages of discount bonds involve their lower price and protection against call, whereas the main disadvantage is associated with capital gains taxes.

Discount bonds allow you to position money in the future that is obtained with a smaller capital outlay today, while at the same time you gather tax-exempt income of your investment. For example, suppose one of your investment objectives calls for a need for money in 15 years. If 15-year bonds with a 5% interest rate are offered in the market to yield 9%, you can purchase these bonds for a dollar price of approximately 67 1/2. You will receive $3 in 15 years for every $2 invested today, and also obtain the tax exempt 5% interest rate during the time you hold the bond. Depending on market alternatives and your tax bracket, the 5% interest rate alone can be very attractive.

Discount bonds protect the investor from bond calls. The issuer of a bond will avoid calling lower coupon bonds whenever possible. If the discount bond should be called, the investor will receive a windfall because the bonds will be called at par or at a premium. Let's look at the previous example of the 5% 15-year bond, selling at a discount. If the bond is priced at 67 1/2, your return is 9% if you hold the bond to its maturity in 15 years. Should the bond be called at par after five years, the accelerated return of your principal makes the yield jump from 9% to more than 14% for the time you held the bond.

The discount bond has a tax disadvantage. The appreciation from the discount price to par at maturity or to a call is subject to capital gains taxes. This tax cuts into the yield you would receive. In making your investment decision, you must know the after capital gains tax yield you will receive on a discount bond. For example, the yield on our discount bond with a 5% interest rate will drop from 9% to approximate 8.6% after a 28% capital gains tax is paid on the appreciation from the 67 1/2 dollar price to 100 at maturity.

When discussing discount bonds, we should also consider the place of zero coupon municipals in the investor's portfolio.

The smaller the coupon on a discount bond, the lower the dollar price. The lowest price on a discount bond is one that has a coupon of zero and pays no interest whatsoever. Much publicity has been given to zero coupon U.S. Treasury bonds where the appreciation in value is taxable. You can also invest in zero coupon bonds issued by municipalities. The appreciation on these bonds from their deep discount price to par at maturity is tax exempt and not subject to capital gains taxes. These bonds are marketed under a variety of different names including zero coupon bonds, multipliers, principal appreciation bonds, and compound interest bonds; I call all these bonds "zeros" because they all have the same general investment characteristics.

How do zeros work? You purchase a $1000 par value zero for an outlay of say $170. If the bond has a maturity of 20 years, the growth of your investment from $170 today to $1000 in 20 years represents a compounded return of approximately 8.75% over the 20 years you held the bond. For the life of the bond however you do not receive any interest income.

The disadvantages of investing in zeros involve their cash flow situation, safety considerations, state tax liability, and poor secondary market.

If you look to your portfolio for cash flow, obviously avoid zeros. When purchasing a zero, look for the highest quality bonds you can find. You are making a long-term bet on the ability of the issuer to have funds available in the future to redeem the bonds, and in the interim you are receiving no income. If the issuer were to default, your investment would have returned you absolutely nothing. Contrast these two situations. In one case, you invest in a 10% bond due in 20 years; after 15 years, the bond issuer defaults. Even if you never see any of your principal again, you at least have the comfort of having received 15 years worth of 10% tax-free interest. If you had invested in a zero with the same unfortunate results, you would show nothing at all for your investment: no interest payments plus a default on the principal. Two types of zeros can be purchased to protect you from this unpleasant happening: zeros insured by top quality municipal bond insurers and zeros backed by Federal Housing Authority insurance programs.

Another disadvantage of zeros arises from the fact that the various states tax each others municipal bonds. If you are a California resident and hold a zero issued by an Arizona municipality, you will find yourself with an annual tax liability to California for the appreciation in value of the Arizona bond. This results in your paying state taxes without the receipt of corresponding revenue, or a negative cash flow on your investment. Obviously, this is an unpleasant situation.

Lastly, the secondary market for zeros is not as good as the secondary market for municipal bonds in general. If you invest in zeros, plan on making them a relatively permanent fixture in your portfolio.

Zeros also have some interesting investment advantages. The primary benefit is the compounding effect. When you purchase a zero, you do not have to take any additional actions with your investment. The bonds are compounding at the return you received at the time of purchase without any reinvestment of interest. The small cash outlay needed to purchase zeros makes them an ideal vehicle for positioning funds in the future for retirement, college costs, or other anticipated needs.

One warning about the low initial purchase price of zeros. Don't invest in zeros just because of their low price. I have seen investors fool themselves into thinking they are millionaires on the basis of holding zeros. You can buy zeros with a maturity value of $1 million for only a fraction of that sum, but that doesn't make you a millionaire until the end of a long, long wait when the bonds mature. This situation is analogous to the investor buying thousands of shares of penny stock: it's not the number of shares you own, it's their value today that counts.

Another misconception about zeros involves their call features. Municipal bonds that are callable can be called at par or at some modest premium; zeros, however, are an exception to this rule. Zeros can be called at various discount prices. Don't invest in zeros and hope for a windfall if the bonds are called: the zeros can be called at substantial discounts from par.

Zero coupon bonds are found offered for sale in the back section of *The Blue List.* You can invest in zeros with various maturities, but the greatest availability and the best investment value tends to be in longer maturities.

LOT SIZE OF HOLDINGS

In managing your bond portfolio, try to keep the number of different lots of bonds to a reasonably low number. All too often individual investors purchase small odd lots of bonds with a resulting portfolio of too many line items of bonds. There is no perfect relationship between the number of different holdings in a portfolio and the overall size, but the following are suggested guidelines:

1. If your portfolio totals $100,000, it should contain no more than four or five different lots of bonds.
2. If your portfolio totals $500,000, it should contain no more than 10 different lots.
3. If your portfolio is more than $1 million, no lot of bonds should be under $100,000.

Excessive lots of bonds have the following disadvantages. First, too many lots result in odd lots which are harder to sell and have less liquidity than round lots. The unit price in the sec-

ondary market is better for 25 bonds ($25,000 par value) than
the unit price for lot sizes under 25 bonds; the best price in the
secondary market would be for lots of 100 bonds or more. Second, there is greater record keeping and processing associated
with large numbers of different bonds without any added benefit
to the portfolio. The task of insuring that interest is received,
checking possible bond calls, and safekeeping the securities becomes unduly complicated and time consuming as the number of
line items increases.

If your investing pattern does not allow you to make such substantial commitments at any one time, consider purchasing dollar bonds or term bonds. In Chapter 3, I discussed the technique
of building a position in one bond issue by making multiple
purchases of the same bond over an extended time. If your purchases will be on the modest size of say $10,000, you should
consider investing in bond funds rather than directly in bonds
themselves.

BOND SWAPPING

Bond swapping plays an important role in municipal bond
portfolio management. Tax exempts are an ideal vehicle for
swapping transactions as there are such a great number of different bond combinations and permutations that make swapping opportunities available. Bonds are swapped to establish paper losses from the portfolio or to restructure the bond portfolio
for changing investment objectives.

With a bond swap, the sale of an existing bond from a portfolio and the purchase of a new bond for the portfolio are accom-
plished in the same market conditions. If you sell bond A and
buy bond B, the value you receive for A and the price you pay for
B should reflect the same market; if the bond market is high or
low, good or bad, hot or cold, a swap makes sense because you
are buying and selling under similar market conditions.

The classic example of a municipal bond swap is the tax swap.

Let's say you purchase $25,000 Nassau County, New York, 5% bonds maturing of July 1, 2005 at par during a period of relatively low interest rates. Time passes and interest rates move upward, resulting in a decline in the market value of your bonds from 100 to 80. There are $25,000 Rockland County, New York, bonds available in the secondary market with a 4 7/8% coupon maturing on January 1, 2005. Because the bonds of Nassau County and Rockland County have similar ratings and because both have approximately the same interest rate and maturity, the market value of each block of bonds in the secondary market will be approximately 80. If you sell your Nassau County bonds and simultaneously buy the Rockland County bonds, what are the results of the bond swap? Figure 12.2 shows that the swap results in a modest $31.25 decline in annual income, but otherwise you find your portfolio in the same general posture both before and after the swap. The important advantage of the swap, however, is the production of a $5000 capital loss on paper resulting from the sale of the Nassau County bonds. An investor can use this loss to reduce current tax liabilities. For simplicity, this example assumes that the bid and asked price on both the bond issues is the same; actually the purchase of the new bonds may be at a price slightly over 80 to cover the dealer's spread in the transaction. This swapping maneuver will result in a capital gain liability if the new bonds are held to maturity because their cost is approximately 80 and will be worth 100 at maturity. The swap works on the principal that the tax write-off now is more beneficial than the tax liability in the future.

FIGURE 12.2. Bond Swap

Investment Position	Before Swap	After Swap
Par value	$25,000	$25,000
Market value	$20,000	$20,000
Bond quality	"A"	"A1"
Maturity	7/1/2005	1/1/2005
Annual cash flow	$1250.00	$1218.75

One word of warning: if you tax swap, avoid a wash sale. Bonds are defined by three factors: the name of the issuer, the coupon rate, and the maturity date. You must have a change in at least two of these three factors to have a legitimate tax swap and not a wash sale. In our example, if you swapped Nassau County 5% bonds for Rockland County 5% bonds of the same maturity, you have a wash sale as only one factor changed, namely the name of the issuer. The Internal Revenue Service would disallow the tax write-off of this transaction because it constitutes a wash sale.

Swapping bonds can achieve other portfolio objectives. Earlier in this chapter we saw an example of a bond swap resulting from an investor's moving from a state with a high income tax to a state without an income tax.

Swapping bonds can restructure the municipal bond portfolio by changing the credit of the holdings. Suppose your portfolio consists mainly of "Baa" and "A" rated bonds. Market conditions on occasion result in bonds of various quality levels trading with narrow yield spreads between them. When this happens, the smart investor swaps out of the lower quality bonds into higher quality. When the spread between the bond quality widens, you reverse the transaction and make a gain for your portfolio. For example, assume that 20-year "A" rated bonds yield 8.10% and that "Aa" rated bonds yield 8.00%; this represents a narrow spread between the bonds of the two rating categories. In dollar terms, the difference between these bonds is about $10.00 per $1000 bond. You swap your lower rated bonds for higher rated bonds. This swap costs you about $10.00 per bond, which is the spread between the two categories. Market conditions change and the spread between "A" and "Aa" widens to 25 basis points; now "A" rated bonds yield 8.25% versus the 8.00% yield for "Aa" bonds. The difference in dollars between the bonds is about $25.00 a bond; you sell your "Aa" bonds and revert to "A" rated bonds, thereby making a profit of $25.00 a bond. The profit is reduced by the $10.00 a bond cost you incurred on the first leg of the swap, but the swap still results in a profit of about $15.00 a bond. The important principle to understand is that this profit can be made regardless of market movements that may have occurred before the initial phase and the final phase of the swap. Because the first buy and sale transaction took place in the same market, and the second buy and sale transaction also took place in the same market—although the second market level could have been very different from the first—the profit results from the spreads between bond quality and not from changes in the market levels themselves.

Swaps also allow quality and maturity changes. If you are concerned about the quality of a bond in your portfolio, swap it for one of different quality. Suppose you are concerned about the quality of the hospital revenue bonds you hold; swap these bonds for some other classification of bonds, for example, water and sewer revenue bonds.

Bond swaps can be used to maneuver against changes in interest rate levels. If you think interest rates are going to decline, swap shorter term bonds for longer term bonds to take advantage of the greater price advance that longer term bonds will experience. If you think rates are going to rise, you should do the opposite: swap long-term bonds for shorter term bonds to protect your portfolio from the dollar decline associated with rising rates.

HIGHLIGHTS CONCERNING PORTFOLIO MANAGEMENT

1. Establish objectives for your planned investments in municipals before calling your bond dealer. Don't let the dealer's inventory set your investment strategy.

2. Don't reduce your overall portfolio returns in an attempt to avoid state taxes.

3. Avoid too many lots of bonds and avoid small lots of bonds under $25,000 whenever possible.

4. Occasionally review your portfolio and your investment objectives. Swap bonds if your objectives change.

5. Don't have a "buy and forget" attitude toward your tax-exempt bonds. Better returns can be obtained from a more active management of a portfolio.

13

taking
the plunge

MAKING THE
SELECTION

We have come to the end of our discussion of municipal securities. We have reviewed how the market functions, types of securities, tax considerations, bond mathematics, and portfolio management. Now the time has come to use this information. Before you make an investment, you must choose both a dealer and the bonds that will go into your portfolio. This chapter will give you some factors to consider when making these choices. I suggest that you re-read this final chapter each and every time you want to invest money in municipal bonds.

CHOOSING THE DEALER

Whether you are making your initial investment in municipal securities or are an experienced investor, the choice of a dealer is an important factor in getting the best possible return from your tax-exempt securities. All dealers are not equal.

If you buy 100 shares of IBM, the price of the stock will be the same regardless of the stockbroker you choose, although there may be slight variations in the commission charge. The stockbroker does not own the IBM stock you are buying; the broker is anxious to see you buy *any* stock as the commission on the transaction forms the stockbroker's profit. By way of comparison, the municipal bond dealer tries to sell you municipal bonds that the dealer actually owns. The profit on the transaction is not in a commission charge but rather in the markup in the price of the bond itself. Markups vary from dealer to dealer; markups range from fair and reasonable in most cases to exuberant in some cases. It is difficult for the individual investor to determine just what are fair market levels and prices for municipal bonds. For this reason, the selection of a dealer is of prime importance.

Here are some guidelines to use in making the selection of a dealer:

1. Choose the municipal bond dealer department of a large brokerage firm or a major commercial bank.

2. If you are using a smaller firm that specializes in municipal bonds, choose a firm that has been in business for a number of years.

3. Ask for recommendations from acquaintances who currently are investing in municipals or from your attorney or accountant.

4. Lastly, and most importantly, use more than one dealer. Call several dealers to compare their offerings and their prices. Shop around. Remember yield to maturity is the key in pricing a municipal bond.

If you are confused about the pricing of municipal bonds or the fairness of a dealer, you should limit your investments to bond funds and to bonds offered in the new issue market at their original issue price.

Never forget when buying or selling a municipal bond that the pricing mechanism is based on a "what the market will bear" philosophy. You are at a decided disadvantage because information about municipal securities is not readily available for the individual investor.

CHOOSING THE BOND

The more thought and discipline you put into the choice of a municipal bond before calling your dealer, the better the selection you will make. Your bond portfolio will be more structured to your personal needs, and your overall investment objectives will be better met. Too many investors buy whatever bond is offered to them by a dealer; over time, their portfolio consists of a series of odd lots of bonds without any direction or structure.

The best way to approach investing in municipal bonds is to ask yourself some questions about your intended bond purchase before making the actual purchase. Here is a check list to review before each and every bond purchase:

1. *Maturity.* When do I want the bonds to mature? How does the maturity of the new bond fit into my current holdings? How does the maturity match my needs for cash in the future? Remember, the longer the maturity, the greater the yield but also the greater the risk. Analyze the municipal yield curve by studying a tombstone ad to see where the best trade-off between risk and reward occurs.

2. *Quality.* With what quality bonds am I comfortable? In general, an "A" rating from both Moody's and Standard & Poor's meets the quality needs of most individual investors. If you want higher quality, consider bonds with credit enhancements that provide extra margins of safety without giving up too much yield. If the yield differential between top quality "AAA" bonds and "A" bonds is less than 30 basis points, choose the higher rated bonds because the differential is narrow and therefore favors the higher rated bond.

3. *State Taxes.* Don't think that you must always invest in the bonds of your state to avoid state taxes and to maximize your tax-free returns. Many times you can buy an out-of-state bond with a high enough return to cover your state tax liability and still provide a higher return than an in-state bond. Determine the yield advantage for your state based upon your state's tax rate and on the interest rate of the bond you are considering purchasing.

4. *Bond Description.* Be sure that you know exactly what the security provisions are for the bond you are considering buying. The description of a bond can be misleading: the large print gives the name of the issuer but the small print tells you exactly what is pledged to pay the principal and interest. Additionally, know what call features are associated with the bond. Insist that your confirmation describe all the possible call features. If the bond is noncallable, this should be noted on the confirmation.

5. *Lot Size.* Depending on the size of your portfolio, try to buy bonds in lot sizes of $25,000 or $100,000 par value. These lot sizes will make your portfolio more manageable and will result in better bids in the secondary market should you wish to sell or swap bonds. If you can not make individual purchases in these sizes, consider buying term bonds that will allow you to purchase matching bonds at a later date in order to have a $25,000 lot, or consider investing in bond funds.

6. *Advertising.* Municipal bonds are advertised like any other product. Although information distributed by municipal bond dealers and their newspaper advertisements help to educate investors, the main purpose of this information and advertising is to sell municipal bonds. Remember, if the yield promised by an advertisement seems too good to be true, it probably is just that.

FUTURE PROSPECTS

The main area to watch in the future is possible changes in the tax codes that might impact the tax exemption of municipal bonds. The Tax Reform Act of 1986 imposed restrictions on issuing certain types of municipal bonds. This will reduce the volume of municipal bonds coming to market in the future, but the effect on individual investors should not be dramatic.

The Tax Reform Act subjects some municipal bond interest to an alternate minimum tax. This is very significant as it represents the first instance of direct taxation of municipal bond interest by the federal government. All investors must be aware of this development and be concerned about the spread of subjecting *all* municipal bond interest to an alternate minimum tax.

Even after the passage of the Tax Reform Act, municipal bonds represent an extremely safe and simple way of avoiding income taxes. With planning before making an investment and with better knowledge of how the market functions, you will be able to receive excellent returns from your municipal investments. And best of all, the money you receive will not have to be shared with tax collectors.

appendix a

BOND AND NOTE
RATINGS

The following are the lettered designations and definitions of municipal bond and note issues used by Moody's and Standard & Poor's. These definitions are reproduced with the permission of Moody's Investors Service and the Standard & Poor's Corporation, from Moody's *Bond Record* and from Standard & Poor's *Bond Guide*.

MOODY'S BOND RATINGS

"Aaa": Bonds that are rated "Aaa" are judged to be of the best quality. They carry the smallest degree of investment risk and are generally referred to as "gilt edge." Interest payments are protected by a large or by an exceptionally stable margin and principal is secure. While the various protective elements are likely to change, such changes as can be visualized are most unlikely to impair the fundamentally strong position of such issues.

"Aa": Bonds which are rated "Aa" are judged to be of high quality by all standards. Together with the "Aaa" group they comprise what are generally known as high grade bonds. They are rated lower than the best bonds because margins of protection may not be as large as in "Aaa" securities or fluctuation of protective elements may be of greater amplitude or there may be other elements present which make the long term risks appear somewhat larger than in "Aaa" securities.

"A": Bonds which are rated "A" possess many favorable investment attributes and are to be considered as upper medium grade obligations. Factors giving security to principal and interest are considered adequate, but elements may be present which suggest a susceptibility to impairment sometime in the future.

"Baa": Bonds which are rated "Baa" are considered as medium grade obligations; i.e., they are neither highly protected nor poorly secured. Interest payments and principal security appear adequate for the present but certain protective elements may be lacking or may be characteristically unreliable over any great length of time. Such bonds lack outstanding investment characteristics and in fact have speculative characteristics as well.

"Ba": Bonds that are rated "Ba" are judged to have speculative elements; their future cannot be considered as well assured. Often the protection of interest and principal payments may be very moderate, and thereby not well safeguarded during both good and bad times over the future. Uncertainty of position characterizes bonds in this class.

"B": Bonds which are rated "B" generally lack characteristics of the desirable investment. Assurance of interest and principal payments or of maintenance of other terms of the contract over any long period of time may be small.

"Caa": Bonds which are rated "Caa" are of poor standing. Such issues may be in default or there may be present elements of danger with respect to principal or interest.

"Ca": Bonds which are rated "Ca" represent obligations which are speculative in a high degree. Such issues are often in default or have other marked shortcomings.

"C": Bonds which are rated "C" are the lowest rated class of bonds, and issues so rated can be regarded as having extremely poor prospects of ever attaining any real investment standing.

"Con.(—)": Bonds for which the security depends upon the completion of some act or the fulfillment of some condition are rated conditionally. These are bonds secured by (a) earnings of projects under construction, (b) earnings of projects unseasoned in operation experience, (c) rentals which begin when facilities are completed, or (d) payments to which some other limiting condition attaches. Parenthetical rating denotes probable credit stature upon completion of construction or elimination of basis of condition.

Note: Those bonds in the "Aa," "A," "Baa," "Ba," and "B" groups, which Moody's believes possess the strongest investment attributes, are designated by the symbols "Aa 1," "A 1," "Baa 1," "Ba 1," and "B 1."

STANDARD & POOR'S MUNICIPAL BOND RATINGS

"AAA": Debt rated "AAA" has the highest rating assigned by Standard & Poor's. Capacity to pay interest and repay principal is extremely strong.

"AA": Debt rated "AA" has a very strong capacity to pay interest and repay principal and differs from the higher rated issues only in small degree.

"A": Debt rated "A" has a strong capacity to pay interest and repay principal, although it is somewhat more susceptible to the adverse effects of changes in circumstances and economic conditions than debt in higher rated categories.

"BBB": Debt rated "BBB" is regarded as having an adequate capacity to pay interest and repay principal. Whereas it normally exhibits adequate protection parameters, adverse economic conditions or changing circumstances are more likely to lead to a weakened capacity to pay interest and repay principal for debt in this category than in higher rated categories.

"BB," "B," "CCC," "CC,": Debt rated "BB," "B," "CCC," and "CC" is regarded, on balance, as predominantly speculative with respect to capacity to pay interest and repay principal in accordance with the terms of the obligation. "BB" indicates the lowest degree of speculation and "CC" the highest degree of speculation. While such debt will likely have some quality and protective characteristics, these are outweighed by large uncertainties or major risk exposures to adverse conditions.

"C": The rating "C" is reserved for income bonds on which no interest is being paid.

"D": Debt rated "D" is in default, and payment of interest and/or repayment of principal is in arrears.

Plus (+) or Minus (−): The ratings from "AA" to "B" may be modified by the addition of a plus or minus sign to show standing within the major rating category.

Provisional Ratings: The letter "p" indicates that the rating is provisional. A provisional rating assumes the successful completion of the project being financed by the debt being rated and indicates the payment of debt service requirements is largely or entirely dependent upon the successful and timely completion of the project. This rating, however, while addressing credit quality subsequent to completion of the project, makes no comment on the likelihood of, or the risk of, default upon failure of such completion. The investor should exercise his own judgment with respect to such likelihood and risk.

MOODY'S MUNICIPAL NOTE RATINGS

MIG 1: Loans bearing this designation are of the best quality, enjoying strong protection from established cash flows of funds for their servicing or from established and broad-based access to the market for refinancing, or both.

MIG 2: Loans bearing this designation are of high quality, with margins of protection ample, although not so large as in the preceding group.

MIG 3: Loans bearing this description are of favorable quality, with all security elements accounted for but lacking the undeniable strength of the preceding grades. Market access for refinancing, in particular, is likely to be less well established.

MIG 4: Loans bearing this designation are of adequate quality, carrying specific risk, but having protection commonly regarded as required of an investment security and not distinctly or predominantly speculative.

STANDARD & POOR'S MUNICIPAL NOTE RATINGS

SP-1: Very strong or strong capacity to pay principal and interest. Those issues determined to possess overwhelming safety characteristics will be given a plus (+) designation.

SP-2: Satisfactory capacity to pay principal and interest.

SP-3: Speculative capacity to pay principal and interest.

appendix b

YIELD AND PRICE FORMULAS
AND EXAMPLES

This appendix shows the formulas that are used for figuring the yield to maturity of muncipal bonds if the dollar price of the transaction is known and for figuring the dollar price if the yield to maturity is known. Each formula is accompanied by an example.

These formulas and examples are reproduced from *Standard Securities Calculation Methods*, published by the Securities Industry Association, New York, 1973, pp. 36–39, with the permission of the publisher.

FORMULA 3
[Yield (given price) with more than six months to maturity]

Note: There is no formula currently available for converting price directly into yield for securities with more than six months to maturity. However, by manipulation of the price formula (using estimated yields) a satisfactory answer can be determined. To accomplish this, an estimated yield is substituted into price formula number four (4). The result of this newly calculated price is then compared to the known price. Based on this comparison, the estimated yield previously substituted into price formula number four (4) is adjusted up or down, as required, to produce a corresponding adjustment in the next price to be calculated. Incremental adjustments are made to the estimated yield until the desired price is matched exactly or within prescribed limits.

Formulas which can be used to approximate a starting yield are shown below. In many cases substituting the interest rate for the yield will provide a satisfactory starting point for the first calculation in the series of calculations necessary. An efficient method for determining the incremental yield adjustments is the Newton method as described in the section entitled "Iteration Theory."

The approximation formulas shown below were developed using approximation methods taken from *Financial Compound Interest and Annuity Tables*, published by the Financial Publishing Company, Boston.

Premium Bonds:

$$Y = \frac{R * NY * 100 - PRM}{(NY * 100) + \left(\dfrac{NY * PRM}{2}\right) + \dfrac{PRM}{4}}$$

Discount Bonds:

$$Y = \frac{R * NY * 100 + DST}{(NY * 100) - \left(\dfrac{NY * DST}{2}\right) - \dfrac{DST}{4}}$$

DST = Discount per $100 par value

NY = Number of years to maturity (as a decimal)

PRM = Premium per $100 par value

R = Annual interest rate (as a decimal)

Y = Approximation of yield to maturity (as a decimal)

Example Formula 3
Municipal Bond

The following example illustrates the calculation of an estimated yield for a municipal bond given a dollar price reflecting a premium.

Settlement Date	2/7/73
Maturity Date	2/1/82
Day Count Basis	30/360
Price = 101.203	$\left(8 + \dfrac{354}{360}\right)$
NY = 8.9833333	

$$PRM = 1.203$$
$$R = 4\frac{1}{2}\% \qquad (0.045)$$
$$*Y = 0.043385366$$

*Actual Yield = 0.043367753
= 4.337%

Example Formula 3
Municipal Bond

The following example illustrates the calculation of an estimated yield for a municipal bond given a dollar price reflecting a discount.

Settlement Date	2/7/73
Maturity Date	8/1/84
Day Count Basis	30/360
Price = 99.525	
DST = 0.475	
NY = 11.4833333	$\left(11 + \frac{174}{360}\right)$
R = 3¼%	(0.0325)
	*Y = 0.032995419

*Actual Yield = 0.032999863
= 3.300%

FORMULA 4
[Price (given yield) with more than six months to maturity]

$$P = \left[\frac{RV}{\left(1 + \frac{Y}{2}\right)_{exp}^{N-1+\frac{DSC}{E}}}\right] +$$

$$\left[\sum_{K=1}^{N} \frac{100 * \frac{R}{2}}{\left(1 + \frac{Y}{2}\right)_{exp} K - 1 + \frac{DSC}{E}} \right] - \left[100 * \frac{R}{2} * \frac{A}{E} \right]$$

A = Number of days from beginning of coupon period to settlement date (accrued days)

DSC = Number of days from settlement date to next six month coupon date

E = Number of days in semi-annual coupon period in which the settlement date falls

exp = Exponential (i.e. term to left of 'exp' is raised to the power indicated by term to the right of 'exp')

K = Defined as summation counter

N = Number of semi-annual coupons payable between settlement date and maturity date or call date if priced to call date (if this number contains a fraction, raise it to the next whole number − i.e. 2½ = 3)

P = Dollar price per $100 par value

R = Annual interest rate (as a decimal)

RV = Redemption value of the security per $100 par value (RV = 100 except in those cases where call features must be considered)

Y = *Annual yield (as a decimal) on investment with security held to maturity or call date if priced to call date

Note: The first term calculates the present value of the redemption amount, not including interest. The second term calculates present values for all future semi-annual coupon payments. The third term calculates the accrued interest agreed to be paid to the seller based upon semi-annual payments.

*Annual yield is also referred to as "Basis" or "Yield Basis."

Example Formula 4
Municipal Bond

The following example illustrates the calculation of a dollar price for a municipal bond, given a yield to maturity, with the settlement date more than six months from maturity.

$$
\begin{aligned}
\text{Settlement Date} \quad & 3/1/73 \\
\text{Maturity Date} \quad & 2/1/83 \\
\text{Day Count Basis} \quad & 30/360 \\
A = (2/1/73 \text{ to } 3/1/73) = \ & 30 \\
DSC = (3/1/73 \text{ to } 8/1/73) = \ & 150 \\
E = (2/1/73 \text{ to } 8/1/73) = \ & 180 \\
N = \ & 20 \\
R = 4\frac{1}{2}\% \quad & (0.045) \\
RV = \ & 100 \\
Y = 4.45\% \quad & (0.0445) \\
P = \ & 100.3939585 \\
\text{Dollar Price} = \ & 100.393
\end{aligned}
$$

appendix c

USING THE BASIS BOOK

Yield	8½ YRS	9 YRS	9½ YRS	10 YRS	10½ YRS	11 YRS	11½ YRS
3.70	109.41	109.87	110.33	110.78	111.23	111.66	112.09
3.75	109.03	109.47	109.91	110.34	110.77	111.18	111.59
3.80	108.65	109.07	109.49	109.91	110.31	110.71	111.10
3.85	108.27	108.68	109.08	109.47	109.86	110.23	110.60
3.90	107.89	108.28	108.66	109.04	109.40	109.76	110.12
3.95	107.52	107.89	108.25	108.61	108.95	109.29	109.63
4.00	107.15	107.50	107.84	108.18	108.51	108.83	109.15
4.05	106.77	107.11	107.43	107.75	108.06	108.37	108.67
4.10	106.40	106.72	107.02	107.32	107.62	107.90	108.19
4.15	106.04	106.33	106.62	106.90	107.18	107.45	107.71
4.20	105.67	105.94	106.21	106.48	106.74	106.99	107.24
4.25	105.30	105.56	105.81	106.06	106.30	106.54	106.77
4.30	104.94	105.18	105.41	105.64	105.86	106.08	106.30
4.35	104.58	104.80	105.01	105.23	105.43	105.63	105.83
4.40	104.22	104.42	104.62	104.81	105.00	105.19	105.37
4.45	103.86	104.04	104.22	104.40	104.57	104.74	104.91
4.50	103.50	103.67	103.83	103.99	104.15	104.30	104.45
4.55	103.14	103.29	103.44	103.58	103.72	103.86	103.99
4.60	102.79	102.92	103.05	103.18	103.30	103.42	103.54
4.65	102.43	102.55	102.66	102.77	102.88	102.99	103.09
4.70	102.08	102.18	102.28	102.37	102.46	102.55	102.64
4.75	101.73	101.81	101.89	101.97	102.05	102.12	102.20
4.80	101.38	101.45	101.51	101.57	101.63	101.69	101.75
4.85	101.03	101.08	101.13	101.18	101.22	101.27	101.31
4.90	100.69	100.72	100.75	100.78	100.81	100.84	100.87
4.95	100.34	100.36	100.38	100.39	100.41	100.42	100.43
5.00	100.00	100.00	100.00	100.00	100.00	100.00	100.00
5.05	99.66	99.64	99.63	99.61	99.60	99.58	99.57
5.10	99.32	99.29	99.25	99.22	99.19	99.17	99.14
5.15	98.98	98.93	98.88	98.84	98.80	98.75	98.71
5.20	98.64	98.58	98.52	98.46	98.40	98.34	98.29
5.25	98.30	98.23	98.15	98.07	98.00	97.93	97.86
5.30	97.97	97.87	97.78	97.69	97.61	97.52	97.44
5.35	97.63	97.53	97.42	97.32	97.22	97.12	97.02
5.40	97.30	97.18	97.06	96.94	96.83	96.71	96.61
5.45	96.97	96.83	96.70	96.57	96.44	96.31	96.19
5.50	96.64	96.49	96.34	96.19	96.05	95.91	95.78
5.55	96.31	96.14	95.98	95.82	95.67	95.52	95.37
5.60 ‹	95.99	95.80	95.63	95.45 ‹	95.29	95.12	94.96
5.65	95.66	95.46	95.27	95.09	94.90	94.73	94.56
5.70	95.34	95.12	94.92	94.72	94.53	94.34	94.15
5.75	95.01	94.79	94.57	94.36	94.15	93.95	93.75
5.80	94.69	94.45	94.22	93.99	93.77	93.56	93.35
5.85	94.37	94.12	93.87	93.63	93.40	93.18	92.96
5.90 ⌝	94.05	93.78	93.53	93.27 ⌝	93.03	92.79	92.56
5.95 ⌟	93.73	93.45	93.18	92.92 ⌟	92.66	92.41	92.17
6.00	93.42	93.12	92.84	92.56	92.29	92.03	91.78
6.10	92.79	92.47	92.16	91.86	91.56	91.28	91.00
6.20	92.16	91.82	91.48	91.16	90.84	90.53	90.24
6.25	91.85	91.49	91.15	90.81	90.48	90.16	89.86
6.30	91.54	91.17	90.81	90.46	90.12	89.79	89.48
6.40	90.93	90.53	90.15	89.78	89.41	89.06	88.73
6.50	90.32	89.90	89.49	89.10	88.71	88.34	87.98
6.60	89.72	89.27	88.84	88.42	88.02	87.63	87.25
6.70	89.12	88.65	88.19	87.75	87.33	86.92	86.52
6.75	88.82	88.34	87.87	87.42	86.99	86.56	86.16
6.80	88.52	88.03	87.55	87.09	86.65	86.22	85.80
6.90	87.93	87.42	86.92	86.44	85.97	85.52	85.09
7.00	87.35	86.81	86.29	85.79	85.30	84.83	84.38
7.50	84.49	83.85	83.23	82.63	82.05	81.50	80.96

Reprinted from *Comprehensive Bond Value Tables*, Publication No. 61, Copyright 1958 by Financial Publishing Company, Boston, MA.

This appendix shows a page from *Comprehensive Bond Value Tables*, Publication No. 61. Copyright 1958 by the Financial Publishing Company, Boston, MA.

Example 1

If you have a bond with a 5% coupon maturing in 10 years, and if the yield to maturity is 6.25%, you can find the dollar price.

1. Go to the section for 5% coupons.
2. Find the correct maturity.
3. Find the yield in the left column.
4. The dollar price is 90.81.

Example 2

For the same 10-year, 5% bond, if the dollar price is 95.45, you can find the yield to maturity.

1. Go to the section for 5% coupons.
2. Find the correct maturity.
3. Find the dollar price under the maturity column.
4. The yield to maturity in the left column is 5.60%.

Example 3 (Interpolation)

Many examples will not have the perfect match of dollar prices and yields; in these cases, you must interpolate to find the approximate answer. With our 5%, 10-year bond, what is the yield to maturity if you purchase this bond at a dollar price of 93?

1. Go to the section for 5% coupons.
2. Find the correct maturity.
3. Find the two dollar prices that band the dollar price of 93 and the yield to maturity for these two dollar prices:

Dollar Price	Yield
93.27	5.90
92.92	5.95

4. Your yield to maturity is between 5.90% and 5.95%.

5. The difference between the dollar prices is .35 (93.27 − 92.92) for a difference of .05 in yield, or .07 difference in dollar price for each .01 in yield.

6. Because your dollar price of 93 is .08 away from the 92.92 dollar price of the 5.95% yield, and because .08 in dollar price is approximately equal to .01 in yield for this example, your yield to maturity is approximately 5.94%.

references

Chapter 1

1. Hilhouse, A. M., *Municipal Bonds: A Century of Experience*, Prentice-Hall, 1936, p 31.
2. Incidents of municipal defaults are not a modern phenomenon. Municipal defaults in the 19th Century were associated with recurring depressions, poor financial practices of carpetbagger governments in the South during the Reconstruction Period, and overzealous municipal support of railroad expansion. The first half of the 20th Century saw defaults in conjunction with land speculation—especially in Florida in the 1920s—and the Depression of the 1930s. For a thorough study of this topic, see Hilhouse, op. cit.
3. The Daily Bond Buyer, *Statistical Handbook*.
4. *Ibid.*
5. The Bond Buyer's 20 Bond Index never exceeded 5.00% until 1969. During the 1950s and 1960s, this index averaged approximately 3.22%.
6. *Readings in American National Government*, edited by Fellman, D. Rinehart & Co., New York, 1947, p 32.
7. *Fundamentals of Municipal Bonds*, Investment Bankers Association of America, Washington, D.C., 1965, p 141.
8. *Ibid.*, p 142.
9. Section 103(a)(1), Internal Revenue Code 1954; quoted ibid., p 141.
10. *Ibid.*, p 144.
11. *Ibid.*, p 141.
12. *Study of State and Local Public Facility Needs and Financing*, Vol. 2, US Government Printing Office, Washington, D.C., 1966, p 322.
13. *The New York Times*, Special Investment Supplement, May, 19, 1985.

Chapter 7

1. Two recent court cases that addressed these areas in favor of the IRS and to the detriment of investors were Earl Drown Corp. v. Comr., No. 3350-82, 86 T. C. No. 15, and Barenholtz v. U.S. No. 85-2250, February 19, 1986.

bibliography

Advisory Committee on Intergovernmental Relations, *State Constitutional and Statutory Restrictions on Local Government Debt,* Advisory Committee, Washington, D.C., 1961.

Advisory Committee on Intergovernmental Relations, *Industrial Development Bond Financing*, Advisory Committee, Washington, D.C., 1963.

Advisory Committee on Intergovernmental Relations, *State Constitutional and Statutory Restrictions on Local Taxing Powers*, Advisory Committee, Washington, D.C., 1962.

American Bankers Association, *A Guide for Developing Municipal Bond Credit Files,* American Bankers Association, New York, 1968.

Center for Capital Market Research, *Planning Designing and Selling General Obligation Bonds in Oregon: A Guide to Local Issuers*, University of Oregon, Eugene, OR, 1978.

Chase Manhattan Bank, *Planning and Marketing A Municipal Bond Issue*, Chase Manhattan Bank, New York, 1963.

Committee on Banking, Finance and Urban Affairs, House of Representatives, Congress of the United States, *Tax Exempt Bonds for Single Family Housing*, US Government Printing Office, Washington, D.C., 1979.

Committee on Finance United States Senate, *Tax Reform Act of 1986*, US Government Printing Office, Washington, D.C., 1986.

Congress of the United States, *Small Issue Industrial Revenue Bonds*, US Government Printing Office, Washington, D.C., 1981.

Connery, R.H., *Municipal Income Taxes*, Proceedings of The Academy of Political Science, Vol. XXVIII, No. 4, Columbia University, New York, 1968.

Curvin, W.S., *A Manual On Municipal Bonds*, Smith, Barney & Co., New York, 1964.

The Daily Bond Buyer, *Preparing a Bond Offering*, The Daily Bond Buyer, New York, 1962.

Darst, D.M., *The Complete Bond Book*, McGraw-Hill, New York, 1975.

Davis, E. H., "*. . . Of the People, By the People, For the People . . .*", John Nuveen & Co., Chicago, 1959.

Debt Rating Services Division of Standard & Poor's Corporation, *Standard & Poor's Rating Guide*, McGraw-Hill, New York, 1979.

Feldstein, S.G., Fabozzi, F.J., Pollock, I.M., Zarb, F.G., (editors), *The Municipal Bond Handbook*, Volumes 1 and 2, Dow Jones-Irwin, Homewood, IL, 1983.

Hempel, G.H., *The Postwar Quality of State and Local Debt*, National Bureau of Economic Research, New York, 1971.

Hilhouse, A.M., *Municipal Bonds: A Century of Experience*, Prentice-Hall, Englewood Cliffs, NJ, 1936.

Homer, S., Leibowitz, M.L., *Inside the Yield Book*, Prentice-Hall, Englewood Cliffs, NJ, 1972.

Homer, S., and Johannesen, R.I., *The Price of Money*, Rutgers University Press, New Brunswick, NJ, 1969.

Hueglin, S.J., and Ward, K. *Guide to State and Local Taxation of Municipal Bonds*, Gabriele, Hueglin & Cashman Inc., New York, 1981.

Joint Economic Committee, Congress of the United States, *State and Local Public Facility Needs and Financing*, Vol. 1 and 2, US Government Printing Office, Washington, D.C., 1966.

Kaufman, H., Hanna, J., *Prospects for Financial Markets in 1986*, Salomon Brothers Inc., 1985.

Kraybill, W.S., *Price Determination of Callable Bonds*, The Chase Manhattan Bank, New York.

Lamb, R., *How to Invest in Municipal Bonds*, Franklin Watts, New York, 1984.

Lamb, R., Rappaport, S.P., *Municipal Bonds*, McGraw-Hill, New York, 1980.

Moody's Investors Service, *Pitfalls in Issuing Municipal Bonds*, Moody's Investors Service Inc., New York, 1977.

Moreland Act Commission, *Restoring Credit and Confidence: A Report to the Governor of the State of New York*, State of New York, Albany, NY, 1976.

Ott, D.J., Meltzer, A.H., *Federal Tax Treatment of State and Local Securities*, The Brookings Institution, Washington, D.C., 1963.

Petersen, J.E., *The Rating Game*, The Twentieth Century Fund, New York, 1974.

Price, R.J., *ABC's of Industrial Development Bonds*, The Packard Press, Philadelphia, 1981.

Public Securities Association, *Fundamentals of Municipal Bonds*, Public Securities Association, New York, 1981.

Rabinowitz, A., *Municipal Bond Finance and Administration*, Wiley-Interscience, New York, 1969.

Smith, W.S., *The Appraisal of Municipal Credit Risk*, Moody's Investors Service Inc., New York, 1979.

Starr, R., *Housing and the Money Market*, Basic Books, New York, 1975.

Tobias, A., *The Only Investment Guide You'll Ever Need*, Harcourt Brace Jovanovich, New York, 1978.

White, W., *The Municipal Bond Market: Basics*, The Financial Press, Jersey City, 1985.

index